*M*ortar *M*atters

*Jesus' encounters with
nine unnamed women*

Jan W. Brown
I Cor. 1:26-29

Jan W. Brown

Mortar Matters

Trilogy Christian Publishers A Wholly Owned Subsidiary of Trinity Broadcasting Network

2442 Michelle Drive Tustin, CA 92780

Cover design by: __

For information about special discounts for bulk purchases, please contact Trilogy Christian Publishing.

Manufactured in the United States of America

10 9 8 7 6 5 4 3 2 1

Library of Congress Cataloging-in-Publication Data is available.

ISBN: 978-1-68556-546-6

E-ISBN: 978-1-68556-547-3

DEDICATION

This book is dedicated to you, the reader. As you read the life stories of these nine unnamed women and consider Jesus' interaction with them, I pray you will gain a renewed sense of His infinite power and boundless compassion. I pray the fervency of His Word will motivate you to impact others near and far until you become a world-reaching woman.

ACKNOWLEDGMENTS

I owe my deepest debt of gratitude to Jerry, my dear husband, for his help and encouragement throughout the entire process of writing *Mortar Matters*. He has supported me through many days and nights of isolation. While writing, he kept me hydrated and nourished, in addition to taking on extra chores. During the COVID lockdown, he motivated me to bring this project to completion.

Steve Crain, friend and gifted writer, was the first to read my manuscript. He offered me assistance with word placement, punctuation, and grammar. His assessment of the content gave me inspiration to complete the task, seek a publisher, bear the cost as a gift to the Lord, and leave the results up to Him.

My earnest appreciation is extended to Maxine Thomas. She, a published writer and dear friend, has given of her time and ability to bring structure to *Mortar Matters*. She has been a delight to work with, always offering positive input. She has been a tremendous source of encouragement to finish the job and to make this message available to the many unknown women in need of its inspiration.

Thank you, thank you, thank you to Carol Plumlee, Dawn Stephens, and Amani White, who saved at least a portion of my sanity as they assisted with computer tasks.

TABLE OF CONTENTS

Dear Reader,

Before you delve into the chapter content of this book, I invite you to find a comfortable place to sit and have a cozy chat with me about the origin and purpose of *Mortar Matters*.

When a small child, I often spent hours outside with my grandmothers as they tended their yards. Each of them had beautiful plants and flowers growing in the spring and summer. Witnessing their love for God's creations plus watching the flowers grow and bloom began an appreciation for the same that has brought joy to me throughout the years.

As a matter of fact, digging in the dirt has become my personal therapy. I find delight in getting outside on a warm day, digging, planting, and attempting to make flowers grow. It was on one of my digging days that the "seeds" of *Mortar Matters* germinated. I was clearing out a spot to plant flowers when I came across some rather strange, red rocks. They were all of the same substance but varied in shape and size. I had never seen anything like them. When I showed them to my husband, he identified them as chunks of mortar. Apparently, when the house was built, the masons allowed the excess mortar to fall to the ground. The landscapers never bothered to clear away the mortar when they planted the bushes around the foundation. Instead, they covered the mortar with topsoil and mulch, leaving the mortar chunks in the ground.

As I unearthed those red rocks, I *saw* the wall in front

of me for the first time. The color combination of the red brick, black shutters, and white trim I found attractive; however, not until that moment did I realize the mortar was red (and red is my favorite color). Still kneeling there on the ground, I wondered *just how* greatly this unnoticed mortar had contributed to the look and, even more importantly, to the structure of my house. Never have I heard mortar complimented when a building was being admired, yet it is essential. Though unnoticed, it is the mortar that holds the walls and the entire building together.

It was an epiphany. There, kneeling on the ground, I realized my life's work paralleled that of mortar. For years, I have been a wife, mother, pastor's wife, paraprofessional, schoolteacher, and grandmother. I have worked in Sunday School, Vacation Bible School, AWANA, summer camps, women's ministries, and more. Most of this was done "between the bricks." Relatively few people know my name or my influence. That is the way life is for many individuals. High-profile people are few compared to the millions and millions of us ordinary folk God created. Why? What is our value? How can we impact our world? Then and there, I remembered that there are numerous individuals in the Bible who remain unnamed. Their stories are recorded for all time. What can we learn from them?

With that thought in mind, I began to search for unnamed women in the New Testament. Oh, that quest has been so enlightening. It has given me a fresh look at

Jesus' ministry. I've seen how He values *one* and uses individuals for His glory, even those that others might consider "nobody." It's been a journey of wonderful insights. Now I want to share some of those with you. I have chosen nine women whose stories were recorded in Scripture, even though their names were never given. As you look at Jesus' interaction with these women, I hope you sense His compassion, mercy, and transforming power and view Him truly as the God-man.

You will notice the word *Selah* is used throughout the book. It's a Bible word used in the Psalms. It simply means "pause and ponder the previous thought."

Dear Reader, I do not claim to be a Bible scholar. Neither are these studies exhaustive. My desire is to take the Scripture truths down off the shelf (so to speak) and, by means of personal examples and applications, make them useful in your everyday life. I have written as if I am your friend, your sister, or your auntie talking and reflecting with you.

For your convenience, at least a portion of the scripture is printed at the beginning of each chapter. Following that, one of my poems that summarizes the story is included. Next is a discussion of the passage with takeaways from each character, then, in conclusion, a prayer.

Mortar Matters was designed to be read *one* chapter at a time. Take your time. Reflect upon the characteristics of Jesus. Read the scripture multiple times. Journal what speaks to you. As you contemplate the personal assessments, consider what concept you can implement into your everyday life. *You,* an unknown woman, are of *great value to our Lord,* and He just may use you to be the *mortar* that *matters*—that cements your friend into God's forever family! That is my prayer.

Okay, let's get started!

Jan.

CHAPTER ONE

THE UNNAMED

Woman at the Well

John 4:3–42

Only selected synoptic scriptures are printed. To get a better understanding of the story, read the entire passage.

> *But He [Jesus] needed to go through Samaria. So He came to a city of Samaria which is called Sychar. ...A woman of Samaria came to draw water. Jesus said to her, "Give Me a drink." ...The woman of Samaria said to Him, "How is it that You, being a Jew, ask a drink from me, a Samaritan woman?" Jesus answered and said to her, "If you knew the gift of God, and who it is who says to you, 'Give Me a drink,' you would have asked Him, and He would have given you living water."*
>
> **John 4:4–5, 7, 9–10**

The Woman at the Well

I came to the well when it was midday,
Hoping to get water, then slip away
Unnoticed by any who would be in that place,
For I was a woman living in disgrace.
What a surprise it was to see
A Jewish man sitting there who spoke to me.
His manner was kind as He asked for a drink.
This was unusual. I didn't know what to think!
He had no vessel or cup in His hand.
He spoke of living water.
I did not understand!
His conversation revealed He knew all about my life,
Even that I had been five different men's wife.
Who could this be who knew my past?
Was it Messiah arrived at last?
Yes! I sensed in my heart and my soul.
Excited, I left my water pot and told
Everyone I could find along the way
It was Jesus, Messiah, I had met that day!

Her Story

In the city of Sychar, at a place called Jacob's Well, the townspeople usually gathered in the cool of the day to draw water for their families. On this day, in the heat of the midday sun, a Samaritan woman arrived carrying her water pot. As she approached the well, she saw a man resting there. He was the first to speak. The man kindly asked her for a drink of water. It was this encounter with a Jewish man that changed her life.

Digging Deeper

The unnamed woman was totally amazed! He was a Jewish man. She detected this by His attire and/or His dialect. The fact that He acknowledged her and spoke to her caught her off guard because Jews and Samaritans were arch-enemies. There was disdain and even hatred between these two people groups. Any self-respecting Jewish man would never make conversation with a Samaritan, and particularly a Samaritan woman. By engaging in conversation with her, the man had crossed ethnic and cultural barriers. At that time, women were not considered equal to men. They were considered inferior beings and treated as such. Yet, neither ethnic nor cultural barriers deterred this man.

The woman registered her surprise at His greeting by pointing out their differences: "You are a Jewish man, and I am a Samaritan woman." The man stated that if she realized with whom she was conversing, she would ask and receive living water from Him, and if she drank of the living water He offered, she would never thirst again. He was speaking of eternal life. She didn't understand, but the statement captured her attention. Of course, she wanted never to thirst again.

"Yes, give me this living water," she responded. Then changing the subject, the man asked her to bring her husband to the well. Oh my, He struck a nerve! "I have no husband," she replied.

The man complimented her honesty and then laid out His knowledge of her past failed marriages, all five of them, as well as her present live-in male companion. The woman's mind was swirling: *Who is this man? How does He know about my past? I've never met Him, yet He has insight into my life. He must be a prophet.*

The man began to speak to her about worship. The methodology. The location. The differences that existed between Jewish and Samaritan worship. When He paused, she confessed that she believed Messiah would come at some point and educate her and others on these things. It was then that the man revealed that He, Jesus, indeed was the Messiah. She had met the promised one, the Messiah! She was astounded by this revelation.

With the excitement of this realization fresh in her heart, she left her waterpot behind and ran to tell others of her encounter with Jesus. As Jesus had encouraged, she brought others back to the well. They listened to His teaching, and many of her fellow Samaritans believed and acknowledged Him as the Messiah. As a matter of fact, these Samaritans were so eager to learn more from Jesus that they persuaded Him to stay in their city for two days longer.

There is a prologue to this woman's story, and it begins with Jesus. Let's backtrack. Jesus had been walking with His disciples from Judea toward Galilee. As mealtime approached, Jesus suddenly announced that He *must go through Samaria*. Knowing the animosity between the Samaritans and the Jews, the disciples wondered *why* He would *want* to go there. They were hungry, and the thought of procuring food took precedence over their curiosity. Off they went to find a meal, leaving Jesus to do as He desired.

Jesus walked until He came to the city of Sychar. Tired and weary from the journey, He found a place to sit down beside a well. He needed rest and refreshment, but these concerns were secondary to His real purpose for going to the well. He knew that one troubled woman would be coming to that precise location. Out of compassion for her, He purposely rearranged His schedule that day to meet her right there! Selah.

Now, let's return to the events surrounding this unnamed woman who came to the well at Sychar. First, she came alone. While other women often walked together, making the chore a bit more congenial, our unnamed woman came alone. At noon. The hottest hour of the day. Why? Probably because she was less likely to meet other women at that time. She chose to be alone. No doubt, she had been the target of gossip, ridicule, finger-pointing, disdain, and contempt from the other women because of her failed marriages. In addition, she had a live-in male friend. News of her infidelity had spread throughout the village. Isolation was her only method of avoiding confrontation and embarrassment.

There are several indications that this woman had some background in Jewish teaching. She knew that Jacob, the Jewish patriarch, had dug and given the well to the people. She was able to discuss worship locations and the worship methods of Jews and Samaritans. She recognized that Jesus' insights were beyond human understanding and, therefore, might indicate that He was a prophet. She concluded that "the man" who spoke to her so kindly could possibly be the long-awaited Messiah. Obviously, seeds of faith had been planted in her spirit. Yet, despite her knowledge, she had made choices that led her into a life of despair, rejection, and heartbreak.

Her heavy water pot is symbolic of the heavy load she brought to the well—a heavy load of hurt, guilt, and shame. By this time of her life, with all that she had experienced, she may have concluded that her poor choices destined her for a lifetime of rejection.

But Jesus came to her, to one hurting individual, specifically to her! He waited for her to arrive. He talked with her, breaking societal norms. His knowledge and compassion touched her heart. He changed her thinking.

He used her to reach out to others. What a difference her one encounter with Jesus made! Selah!

In this narrative, we see Jesus as Emmanuel, God with us. This concept is far beyond our finite comprehension. How could God the Son be compressed into humanity? It had never happened before and has not happened since. Yet, in this passage, we see Jesus as fully human and fully God. We see His humanity as He was walking with His disciples, growing tired from the journey, resting at the well, and desiring refreshing water. We see Him as God when He showed up exactly where the woman was to come and when He knew of her past marriages and her present live-in situation. We see Him not intimidated by the restrictions of man as He crossed cultural barriers to meet the woman and her needs. Their time together brought about transformation in her thoughts and desires. His words and actions show us that nothing was beyond His ability. Jesus was Emmanuel, God with us! Selah!

Jesus knows the pain of divorce. He understands that two individuals cannot be joined in life, in spirit, and in body, then separate without experiencing deep emotional pain. This woman had been divorced five times. She had given her heart, her emotions, and her body to five men, only to be rejected by each of them. Apparently, the pain was so intense that she gave up on marriage, but needing support and companionship, she settled for cohabiting with man number six. Jesus was fully aware of the trauma and scars she carried. He came to her with compassion, leaving behind His disciples and His *plan A* for the day to

21

venture into *enemy territory* to meet her where she was. He came to her as *man number seven*. In the Bible, seven is considered the number of completion. This goes all the way back to creation. God, our Creator, finished His work of creation on day six and then rested on the seventh day, not because of exhaustion but completion.

Unannounced on this day, Jesus came as man number seven, the completer, to replace hurt with peace and to replace turmoil with rest for one lonely woman. He took time and effort to walk extra miles, to open the eyes of her understanding, and to fill her heart with joy. What a day to be in Samaria by the well at Sychar! Selah!

Jesus used the metaphor of life-giving water to draw a parallel to His truth. Just as one receives nutrients and refreshment from clean water, so are we fed from the Word of God. It is pure. It is satisfying. It cleanses. We just need to ingest it intentionally. Daily, as we spend priority time in the Word of God, life is imparted into our souls. Much like a spring from deep inside the earth, it is refreshing, nourishing, and never runs dry. Mankind has attempted to fill his empty soul with many other things such as achievement, fame, alcohol, sexual pleasures, entertainment, and so much more. These are temporary pleasures. Yes, these bring momentary relief from the gnawing emptiness felt deep within. It is Jesus and the truth found in His Word that bring lasting satisfaction. The writer of the song "Satisfied" expressed this concept so well.

All my lifelong I had panted
For a draught from some cool spring,
That I hoped would quench the burning
Of the thirst I felt within.
...Feeding on the husks around me,
Till my strength was almost gone,
Longed my soul for something better,
Only still to hunger on.
Poor I was, and sought for riches,
Something that would satisfy,
But the dust I gathered round me
Only mocked my soul's sad cry.
Well of water, ever springing,
Bread of life, so rich and free,
Untold wealth that never faileth,
My Redeemer is to me.
Hallelujah, I have found Him
Whom my soul so long has craved!
Jesus satisfies my longings;
Through His life I now am saved.
(Public domain)

What lessons can we learn from this woman's encounter with Jesus?

- **Jesus Went the Extra Mile**

  He left His disciples, His comfort zone, to meet the need of one individual. This woman may have been considered hopeless or even worthless by others. Not to Jesus. Although He knew her troubled past, He had compassion for her and saw her future potential. How do you and I measure up to this example? Are we willing to break from the comfort of family and friends to care for someone outside of our ethnic, cultural, or socioeconomic group? Are we willing to be inconvenienced or to change our schedules to bring hope to those viewed by others as hopeless? As we grow in Jesus' likeness, we will become more and more comfortable in going beyond our comfort zone.

- **Jesus Offered Eternal Life**

  He offered the unnamed woman living water that would be like a fountain continually springing up inside her. What a beautiful word picture! Her soul went from dry and thirsty to full and overflowing. In this brief passage of scripture, we see the change from rejection and isolation to an enthusiastic outpouring of joy spreading to many of her fellow countrymen.

  This one encounter with Jesus brought a

complete change in our unnamed woman's direction and desires. She went from *hiding* from others to boldly *seeking* others to tell them of Jesus' teaching at the well. Her story shows us that there is no situation or person beyond our Lord's capacity to change.

Nothing (that is no thing) is impossible with God.

Perhaps while reading this account, you find yourself identifying with this woman. You may have made a negative decision or many of them that plummeted you into a life you never wanted or intended. Like this unnamed woman, your situation is not beyond the reach of our Lord. Several times the Bible clearly states that nothing is impossible with Jesus. He is sitting by your well, waiting for you to come to Him. He is willing to forgive you, transform you, and use you, warts and all, to bring honor to Himself. Cry out to Him. He will be there for you. He will give you living water, eternal life, which will bring a total life change to you. He can change your actions, desires, and direction just as He did for this unnamed woman who came to the well. It doesn't matter where you have been or what you have wandered into; you can be delivered. There is absolutely no situation too difficult for the Lord to forgive, cleanse, and transform.

Jesus came to this unidentified woman personally and intentionally, face to face! Now that He has ascended, He has left His Holy Spirit and His Holy Word to teach and guide us. While the written Word of God was not available to her, we are privileged that it is readily accessible to us. It is our source of living water. Its truth is inexhaustible. The more we read a passage, the more truth we begin to understand. Yet, the next time we read the exact words, we discover another aspect of its teaching. As we consistently select a few verses to read, reread, ponder and even memorize, their truth becomes buried deep in the well of our soul. They become part of us. Then as we walk through life's varied situations, they spring up from our well, bringing comfort and guidance into our own life as well as to those around us.

- **Jesus Arrived First, Purposefully**

Jesus anticipated the woman's arrival. Knowing her personal pain, He came specifically to meet her. He was eager to give her peace, forgiveness, and a new focus on life. He arranged His schedule with the intention of meeting the need of one troubled, socially outcast woman.

In His omniscience, Jesus knew she would arrive. But consider what she would have missed if she had not come to the well that day. I wonder how many times Jesus has come to sit by the well of His Word waiting for me (or you) to come and drink from the everlasting water of life…but I (you) stood Him up? We have no way of knowing what we experienced as a result of neglecting our time to meet with Jesus. It could have been guidance from the Holy Spirit, a loving message from the Scripture, peace in a trial, an answer to a prayer, ideas for reaching out to others, freedom from confusion, and so much more. Those opportunities are gone. Going forward, let's determine never to leave Jesus sitting at the well awaiting our communion with Him. Selah!

- **No One Is Beyond Hope**

This passage shows us that no one is too messed up to be transformed and even used by God. Jesus looked beyond the unnamed woman's past filled with negative decisions and disappointments. He realized and focused on her potential. Regardless of where her past had taken her, He knew her future. With forgiveness and everlasting life continually springing up from within her soul, the remainder of her life could be devoted to following Jesus and bringing many of her own people, the Samaritans, to new life in Him.

It appears that seeds of truth previously had been sown into this woman's life. We don't know by whom or how far in her past. This should serve as encouragement for us today. Sometimes we Christians drop seeds of the Word into the lives of our friends or family members. We watch for progress and end up feeling like failures when there is no evidence of growth. Be encouraged! We have no idea when the Holy Spirit will bring life to those seeds and completely transform our loved ones. We must keep scattering seeds and never give up. No one is beyond hope. Selah.

Remember that no one is beyond hope.

We have no way of knowing how far this woman's influence reached. The Bible tells us that she brought many with her back to the well. We can assume that at least some of them brought others to Jesus. Those, in turn, brought others, and so goes the ripple effect. All this began with the testimony of one most unlikely, unnamed woman that Jesus needed to go through Samaria to reach and whose life was changed by one encounter with Him.

Personal Response

1. Like Jesus, how likely are you to "go the extra mile" to reach out to a troubled individual, even one outside your comfort zone?

       1   2   3   4   5

2. Bit by bit, read and ponder the Word of God. Listen for His message to you. Document those insights in a journal. Try never to leave Jesus sitting by your well, waiting to speak to you.

3. Choose some brief passages to run deep into *your well* that will become springs of living water to others. Start with one verse or familiar passage such as John 3:16; Psalm 23; Psalm 1. Concentrate on that one verse or passage until it is your own, buried deep into the well of your soul.

4. Remember that no one or no situation is beyond hope. With God *all* things are *possible*! Write the name of the person or situation in your life that presently appears impossible.

   _____

5. Keep dropping seeds of truth, love, and encouragement. You have no idea when those will

spring up and bring new life into another person. Never give up! Commit now: I will continue to reach out to _____

6. Take time to meditate on these personal considerations. Pray about your spiritual influence on others. Then write an action plan for implementing any of these concepts that need improvement.

Prayer

Lord Jesus, I thank You for the words of life for me to read and understand in this story. Thank You for demonstrating how compassion and going the extra mile look. Thank You for showing me the high value You place on one individual. I want to follow Your example. Teach me how to be Your disciple as I meditate on portions of Your Word. I never want to leave You sitting at the well of my heart, awaiting my arrival. I need Your direction. Show me what person around me needs Your words springing up from my well. Give me courage to speak truth to him or her. My desire is to walk in Your ways. I am weak. Strengthen me every day. Amen.

Afterword

While studying this biblical narrative, I thought about the value of water in our everyday lives and how we take it for granted. Water is essential to the existence of all living things, both animals and plants. It is so vital that God, our Creator, covered two-thirds of the earth's surface with water. More than fifty percent of the human body is composed of water. When teaching the importance of water to small children, I used to tease them, saying, "If I could squeeze all the water out of you, you would only be *this big*." My little chickadees found that to be interesting and amusing.

In America, we are blessed to have clean, drinkable water in abundance. We have water in multiple rooms of our homes. There are bathrooms and water fountains in almost all businesses. Clean, running water is a natural part of our everyday life. With the twist of a faucet, we can take a shower, make a drink, water our plants, flush toilets, soak off baked-on foods, wash clothes, and much more.

While water from faucets is a blessing, rain is an even greater blessing. When God pours down non-chemically treated water for our grass, trees, and flowers, our gardens flourish. The air is refreshed. Even the heat of the day becomes tolerable.

With water being so readily available to us, we might not appreciate the significance of a well in biblical times. We cannot imagine trudging miles to a common well in the middle of a city while carrying a clay pot, a pot that is heavy even when it is empty. Walking back home with that filled pot on our shoulders or head would be quite burdensome. It is a foreign concept to us but still commonplace in many places in the world. It was the norm in Jesus' time.

Oh, how blessed we are today!

CHAPTER TWO

THE UNNAMED

*Widow Who
Gave Her All*

Now Jesus sat opposite the treasury and saw how the people put money into the treasury. And many who were rich put in much. Then one poor widow came and threw in two mites, which make a quadrans. So He called His disciples to Himself and said to them, "Assuredly, I say to you that this poor widow has put in more than all those who have given to the treasury; for they all put in out of their abundance, but she out of her poverty put in all that she had, her whole livelihood."

Mark 12:41–44

The Widow's Mite

A widow came to the temple to worship the Lord,
To give honor and praise to the one she adored.
Two tiny coins were all that she had
When placed in the offering, they made Jesus glad.
The value of the money was so very small,
But what got His attention was she gave her all.
Yes, all that she had of the world's goods
She released to the Lord, as few people would.
With pomp and flair, others gave much more
As they called attention to themselves and the clothes
they wore.
A gasp, a clap, an adoring look,
For a moment in time was all that they took.
But the widow whose name we don't even know
Was noticed by Jesus for the gift she did sow.
He saw the gift that seemed oh so small,
Recorded it in Mark and Luke for us all,
To remind us that it's not the size of the gift we bring,
But a heart filled with worship is the important thing.

Her Story

When we met this unnamed woman, known only as the widow who gave two mites, she was in the house of worship. It was offering time when Jesus arrived at the synagogue. There He observed those who were making contributions. Perhaps it was what we would consider a "march offering" where everyone who desired to give walked past the treasury, dropped in their contribution, then returned to their place of worship. Jesus saw numerous well-dressed individuals pompously walk by and deposit large sums of money. These persons did not impress Him. It was one poor widow who had very little to give that captured Jesus' attention. It was from her generosity that He chose to teach us about giving. Although her gift was almost worthless, from a heart of worship, she gave all.

Digging Deeper

One, *Poor*, *Widow*. These three words give us our only insight into the life of this unnamed woman. Let's consider each word, but not necessarily in the order given in Scripture. First, *she was a widow*. That tells us she had experienced or was still going through one of the most difficult stressors of life: the loss of a spouse. She had faced heartbreak, grief, and overwhelming devastation. She had to make personal adjustments in every aspect of her life, including family relationships, financial expectations, social acceptance, and much more.

A young widow once expressed to me that becoming a widow was like having an amputation. Part of you is gone! You can survive, but life will never be the same. As with physical amputation, one can survive without one's mate. Physically, a prosthetic limb can be used to replace a missing limb, but adjusting to it is a slow, painful process. Becoming a widow draws a close parallel. Adjusting to life without a spouse is also a slow and painful process. As difficult as it is to be a widow today, it was far more burdensome in Bible times. Unlike today, women then did not typically hold money-producing jobs. Therefore, when a husband died, so did the widow's source of income. Life was hard. No pension. No Social Security. Real poverty ensued.

Second, *she was poor*. The word *poor* immediately conjures up several mental images. To a poor woman living in America, it might mean rinsing and reusing paper cups and plates, eating less so that the meal will stretch around the table, and pinching pennies until they squeal. To someone living in a third-world country, the situation is often much worse. Think of adults and children pillaging through garbage dumps seeking scraps of food to eat or tin cans or bottles for resale. That is truly poor and much more like the abject poverty this widow faced. Our unnamed widow was down to her last two coins, each one of less value than a penny. After she contributed both coins, she had little possibility of a financial turnaround. She was headed for a permanent state of being hopelessly poor.

The third descriptive word, *one*, tells us she was alone at the temple that day. She had no family member or friend with whom to share her worship experience. We can imagine this lady timidly deposited her gift in a way that did not attract attention to herself; that in comparison to the others nearby who flamboyantly threw large sums of money into the treasury. That's one view. On the other hand, she may have been so caught up in worship experience at that moment that she impulsively emptied her finances to God. Either way, her goal was to be quiet, unobtrusive, without anyone taking notice of her. This poor widow was alone, going through heartbreak, and down to her last cent. Did anyone else realize that? Maybe not.

To me, being alone is sad. Ever since I was a toddler, I have wanted to have people around me. Now in my adult years, I am still most joyful and fulfilled when there are people around. Jerry and I love having folk over for a meal, a family gathering or celebration, or a church event. The more who come, the better we like it. I realize that not all people get that kind of satisfaction out of hospitality, and I respect that. However, the point at hand is we need to seek out the lonely. We need to include and befriend them. While this brings encouragement into their lives, the joy of giving also spills over into our lives as well.

Earlier, Jesus had been talking to His followers about the arrogance of the scribes and Pharisees, the religious leaders of that day. He told how these people made themselves known by flaunting their long robes and assuming seats of honor in the synagogue, in the marketplace, and at public feasts. They dishonored widows. They prayed bold, loud prayers to be heard of men. Jesus saw the hearts and motives of these self-absorbed individuals. He was not impressed.

He went into the synagogue to meet with some of His followers to teach more of His new theology of peace, grace, and forgiveness. When He arrived, He observed the offering being given. There He saw quite a contrast between the wealthy dropping a "token" into the treasury and the poor widow who quietly deposited *all she* possessed. It was her tiny gift that He had recorded in the New Testament. Jesus saw *her* giving, and He saw *her* heart. It was not the amount she gave but the fact this *one poor widow* gave all she had.

All she had! Although her all was worth almost zero, it was her heart of worship that honored Jesus. Despite her circumstances, this woman had chosen to be a worshiper that day. She wanted to hear the Scriptures read by the rabbi. She wanted to pray and give what she could. Her self-talk could have convinced her that those two coins were not enough to make a difference in the life of anyone else. Perhaps if she kept one for herself, she could avoid becoming *dead broke*, but she chose to give all. Her gift caused Jesus to draw a sharp contrast between her gift and the gifts of the rich. To Jesus, her *all*, although almost worthless, was of greater value than the tip given from the wealthy out of their affluence. Selah.

Giving all can be a deed or an attitude. Years ago, I used James 1:17 as the basis for a workshop at a women's retreat. "Every good gift and every perfect gift is from above, and comes down from the Father of lights, with whom there is no variation or shadow of turning" (James 1:17). Everything we have is from His benevolent hand. We should consciously use and enjoy His gifts, yet never be obsessed or controlled by them. When we are not grasping and grabbing, we can tenderly unfold our fingers to share with others from His blessings to us.

When prompted by the Holy Spirit of God, all our time, talent, and treasure should be available for His use. Our hands should never be clasped so tightly that giving would become painful if resources have to be pried away from us. Out of gratitude for our abundance, we should keep our hearts and hands open before the Lord. We must be willing to share anything at His call. This attitude of having all available to the Lord reminds me of a song we sang in my home church when I was a child. "Fully Surrendered" is written with some old English terms, but I think the message is clear:

Fully surrendered—Lord, I would be,

Fully surrendered, dear Lord, to Thee.

All on the altar laid,

Surrender fully made,

Thou hast my ransom paid;

I yield to Thee.

Fully surrendered—life, time, and all,

All Thou hast given me held at Thy call.

Speak but the word to me,

Gladly I'll follow Thee,

Now and eternally,

Obey my Lord.

(Public domain)

Our unnamed widow was down to her last two coins. After she contributed both of them, she had little possibility of a financial turnaround. She was heading for a permanent state of discouragement and being helplessly poor. Yet, I strongly suspect that after her encounter with Jesus, this woman had miraculous provision. The Bible teaches in both the Old and the New Testaments that God promises unusual provision for those who dare to be givers. Look into Malachi 3:10–11, Matthew 6:33, and Luke 6:38. Each of these passages shows that God is blessed by the giving of His people. When we are generous, He keeps the supply coming, thereby enabling His people to give again and again. The last time I read through the Bible, a concept that surfaced time and time again was "God is continually giving." That is His nature. He is pleased when His children mimic His giving attribute. Take a few minutes to contemplate the promises and protections He offers to givers stated in these verses. These are the reasons, in my opinion, that there had to be a connection between this one day in this woman's life and the provisions that came in her future.

My husband, Jerry, has a pastor friend who was challenged to give his all. At the time he was called into full-time pastoral ministry, he was already married, had children, and was well established in a profitable business. To prepare for ministry, he had to take giant steps of faith by selling his house, leaving his secure job, and taking his entire family into the college scene. Those were not easy years, yet he and his family experienced the Lord's faithful provision. They made it through those lean years. For decades since, he and his family have been used to relate to many others the faithfulness of God to those who dare to step out in obedience. They learned firsthand the truth of this quotation. Where He guides, He provides.

Where He guides, He provides!"

As we view our God as all-knowing and all-powerful, we will grow in our understanding that He has more means and ideas of caring for His children than we can imagine.

Jerry and I learned this lesson quite a few years ago. Our first pastorate was in a small church in a small town in Florida. The starting salary was $156 per week. (I have no idea how the church decided on that amount. Not $155 or $160, but $156.) That was for four of us. Our two children were young at that time, so I was not working outside the home. I was heavily involved in ministry side-by-side with my husband.

Back in those days, somewhere around 1979–1980, it was customary for all area clergy to participate in dinners that were planned to promote any ministry or crusade coming to town. Jerry and I attended a mission presentation. It was compelling and touched our hearts deeply. We wanted to give, but what? We tithed from our income. We gave to our denominational missions program. How could we give more with so little left over? After whispering back and forth, we decided to give twenty dollars.

Twenty dollars was our food budget for the week and about all the discretionary money we had. We had no idea how this was going to work, but we trusted that the Lord had a plan. The following week, our little family received invitations for a meal from four of our church families. That has never happened before or since in our forty-one years in ministry. It was God showing up and showing out. He was proving His care and provision for His children. I think we ate better that week with others than we would have from the twenty dollars we gave away. Jehovah Jireh! Truly, He is our provider. Each of the four families that reached out to us had been nudged by the Holy Spirit to invite us to dinner. Not any one of them had any idea that God would show Himself strong to us through their generosity.

With that in mind, I challenge you, as I challenge myself, to respond in obedience any time God nudges. Let's not procrastinate. Let's not say no. Doing so will rob the receiver as well as ourselves of the blessing. It is impossible to follow the Spirit's leading to meet the need of someone else without being deeply touched and encouraged ourselves. I am so glad these people said "yes" to the Lord. They gave in to the nudges of the Holy Spirit, and forty years later, I am still recalling God's provision for us through their obedience and generosity.

Some people feel uncomfortable when giving is discussed. They express the "all they want is my money" attitude. Not true. Giving is not a punishment. It should be a joy. Think of the privilege it is to partner with the Lord of heaven to spread His truth and help to others. Selah! The Bible tells us, "It is more blessed to give than to receive" (Acts 20:35). After experiencing life on both sides of that statement, I have concluded that it is more blessed to be *able* to give than to *have* to receive. If we take an honest look at our possessions, we will see that we are *able* to give. Often, we are guilty of taking our abundance for granted. We are used to having more than enough. Rather than expressing gratitude to the Lord for all our blessings, we tend to compare what we have with others who possess more.

45

We need to count our blessings every day. I challenge you to take a one-minute break *right now* and write down as many blessings as you can within that time frame. Look at your watch. Go ahead. Take a gratitude minute. When we take an honest assessment, it is difficult to stop listing our blessings after such a short time. Perhaps we should challenge ourselves to take a gratitude minute every day for a week or a month. Remember, thanksgiving is not one day a year or even a season. It should be our way of life. The more we discipline ourselves to give thanks to our Father, the more we will be conscious of our blessings. Out of the abundance we possess, we can joyfully give to others without thinking, *Do I have to?*

Giving begins with gratitude and then priority. Jesus tells us in Matthew 6:33, "But seek first the kingdom of God and His righteousness, and all these things [the essentials of life] shall be added to you."

How do we flesh this out? First, we settle the issue that God does not need our stuff. He created the entire universe. He provides for and manages it quite well. What He desires is that His children love and honor Him supremely. He wants us to be so in tune with His will and His ways that we lovingly and willingly give to Him and others first. How? Give Him the first moments of our day. Even before crawling out of bed, send up a prayer of thanksgiving, then commit the day to Him. Ask Him to use you to bring light and life into someone's day. You might have your *to-do* list but tell Him that He is welcome to change your activities as He chooses. His choices come first.

Another way to seek His kingdom first is to give Him the first day of the week. At creation, God established the work-six, rest-one pattern. Sunday is our day of rest and should be different from days two through six. That doesn't mean we must spend twenty-four hours in church or on our knees. Certainly, these things should be included. As we worship, rest, and put aside the demands of the workday world to refresh our minds and bodies in a less stressful setting, we can have a more productive work week than ever before. Give God the first day of your week. His ways cannot be improved upon. Six days to work and stress. One day to worship and rest.

> *Six days to work and stress.*
> *One day to worship and rest.*

Prioritizing our giving is another way to put God first. To me, that means writing my giving checks first. We all know if we wait until last or until we have "enough," giving just won't happen. But when we give our ten percent (or whatever amount you are presently committed to giving), it sanctifies the remainder to go farther. It truly does. Selah!

We learned a giving concept at a wonderful church we attended in Norfolk, Virginia, long ago when Jerry was in the Navy. The idea was that when we give of our earnings, it is like taking work hours and rolling them into a check, thus giving of ourselves to the Lord. You and I might not be able to preach a sermon, go to Uganda or India, or build an orphanage, but our work hours squeezed into a check can enable others to do those exact things. What a privilege! We can become world-reaching women right from our own homes. This not only blesses others here and abroad but fills our lives with purpose. We are a part of what God is doing worldwide. We don't have to give; we get to. It's our privilege!

> *We don't have to give.*
> *We get to.*
> *It's our privilege!*

We need to follow these gifts with prayer, asking God to direct the $10, $20, $50, or $100 to just the right person. I have witnessed this happen many times as giver and receiver. Almost everyone involved in American Christianity is familiar with Samaritan's Purse Shoebox Project. What began as a good idea for reaching impoverished children at Christmas has evolved into an outreach to millions of children annually. Personally, I don't know anyone who can pack a million boxes, yet each person involved can pack one box, two boxes, or more. As we make purchases, we must ask for the Spirit's guidance so that our box can bring extreme joy plus a sense of God's love to a specific child. I have read how the right toy, color of items, and even tools were used to bring untold delight to individuals and families. One story was told of a family whose father's tools had either been stolen or lost in a natural disaster. He needed tools to provide for his family. A person, thousands of miles away, was impressed to put hand tools in a shoebox gift. The packers almost pulled the tools since that is not what is normally sent to a child for Christmas. The tools were not pulled but got to the right family at the right place. Both the child and the father were overwhelmed by God's provision. Selah!

Pray for your giving to be an instrument in the Father's hand, whether it is money or some other commodity. The item or the amount does not matter. Anything can be used in ways only heaven will reveal. Surrender your giving by praying over its impact. Just as Jesus observed the widow's offering and used her story down through the centuries, so He does today. He is aware of what we *give* as well as what we *keep*.

He is aware of our attitude as well. The Bible states that He loves a cheerful giver. We grow into cheerful giving as we begin with the discipline of systematic giving. We give first and don't waver. The more systematically we give, and the more aware we become of the impact our giving has on others, the more cheerfulness will grow within us.

What can we take away from each of the characters in this brief passage?

The Rich

They had plenty. From Jesus' description, they were prideful and condescending. There is no indication that He rebuked them. They were allowed to enjoy their abundance and the fleeting moment of man's acknowledgment. Certainly, not all wealthy people are selfish by nature. Jerry and I have met persons of great means who were extremely generous givers. Much of their giving was done anonymously. They perceived themselves to be blessed in order to be a blessing.

The rich people in the synagogue apparently were not mindful of others who were not like themselves, that is, those with meager means, hurting or alone. I wonder how often you and I walk past a person who is hurting, lonely, and in need of a friendly gesture. Probably more often than we realize. Most of us have been in a new, unfamiliar setting at one time or another, so we know how difficult it is to be "a stranger." Although there may be people all around, the new person is keenly aware of being the outsider. The challenge we face is to be sensitive to the newcomer, the newly widowed, or the stranger in our life setting. Ask the Lord to show you who in your world is experiencing isolation or loneliness. Ask Him what you can do to make that person feel welcome. It might be something as simple as sending a text message, a phone call, giving one flower, one muffin, or any other small gesture.

Even the smallest remembrance can bring a ray of light, a smile, and a sense of value to a person who feels isolated. One deed can bring a flicker of hope into a day of despair or rejection. Who knows, it could be just the *mortar that matters* to build a new relationship. This act of kindness could be remembered for a lifetime or even signal the beginning of a forever friendship.

The Widow

She meekly came to worship despite her circumstances. While she did not have the clothing or the offering of those around her, she had a desire to learn and participate at the temple. I doubt she ever knew Jesus was watching. Assuredly, she was unaware that her humble deed would be recorded for future generations. Her tiny gift proved the truth in one of my mother's favorite songs:

"Little is Much When God Is In It."

In the harvest field now ripened
There's a work for all to do;
Hark! The voice of God is calling
To the harvest calling you.
Does the place you're called to labor
Seem too small and little known?
It is great if God is in it,
And He'll not forget His own.
When the conflict here is ended
And our race on Earth is run,
He will say, if we are faithful,
"Welcome home, My child, well done!"
Little is much when God is in it,
Labor not for wealth or fame;
There's a crown, and you can win it,
If you go in Jesus' name.
(Public domain)

From her easy chair in the den, my mother quietly lived out the principle in this song she loved. She prayed for family, friends, and outreach. As long as she was able, she shopped (her hobby) for items for her church's missionary closet. For years she cut and trimmed stamps for her church's stamp project. (Incidentally, they raised thousands of dollars annually by reselling canceled stamps). She would buy commemorative stamps. Whenever she sent me a letter, she would write "save stamp" on the envelope. There, alone in her chair, she also wrote checks. When my sister took over Mother's finances, she was shocked to learn the portion of her income Mother gave away. Read the words to her favorite song again. Giving brought her joy and purpose. Her motto was: "Do your giving while you are living, so you are knowing where it is going."

The Lord

Throughout the New Testament, Jesus was drawn to the needy, the unknown, and the lonely. He sees and knows everything! On this day, it was the obscure, hurting woman that got His focus. He chose to look beyond her poverty and pain. He chose to value her "little." To others, she may have been a nobody. Not to Jesus. He placed great value on her and her actions.

He did not gravitate to the popular people, the accepted, the ones who seemed to "have it all together." Instead, He sought out the underdog, the hurting, and the poor. So, when you feel small, unnoticed, or insignificant, be encouraged. That is just the type of person Jesus is drawn toward. Just like this *one poor widow*, you are also of incalculable value to Him. He knows you, where you are, your name, and even the number of hairs on your head. Selah! (Did you ever try to count your hairs?)

In this case, Jesus had this woman's seemingly insignificant story recorded in the Gospels of both Mark and Luke. For the centuries that have followed, millions have read of her worship and her generosity. This one poor widow has been an inspiration to countless individuals. Oh, how Jesus valued this one unknown individual. Shouldn't we go about our daily lives doing the same?

A Personal Reflection

Every time I hear the word *generosity*, I remember my aunt Hazel. Her name is synonymous with generosity in my mind. Aunt Hazel was divorced many years ago when divorce was discussed only in hushed circles. Life was not easy for Aunt Hazel and her young daughter. Yet, with hard work and careful money management, she and her daughter were dressed and provided for as nicely as any two-parent family. Throughout the years, Aunt Hazel worked at department stores in downtown Atlanta. I feel certain her income was considerably less than a dollar per hour.

Aunt Hazel never owned a car, so she had to live near the bus line. I will never understand how she was able to purchase a house. Yet she did. It was a house with an apartment which was a financial asset so long as renters were present. As a child, I thought she was well-off. After all, she wore nail polish, makeup, and jewelry. My mom never wore nail polish and very little makeup or jewelry (by preference, not because of any religious conviction).

Not only did Aunt Hazel dress with a little bling, but she blessed everyone around her. She was a giver! She had an exceptional way of making a gourmet meal by cleaning out the refrigerator. Everything was delicious, and it was presented with a beautiful flair. She absolutely loved sharing what she had with others. She gave elegant showers, parties, and family gatherings. I would venture to say that every lady in her church owned something made by her generous hands—and hers was not a small church. The gift might be booties, a sweater, or a blanket for a baby. It could be an Afghan, a cape, or a knitted scarf for an adult. Since she was constantly learning new crafts, a gift could have been one of a countless number of items lovingly crafted by her industrious and generous hands.

As Aunt Hazel grew into her senior years, my parents attempted to help her, but she turned everything that was given to her into an item of beauty and then gave it away to someone else. Her generosity, creativity, and frugality left a lasting impression on me. In a world where the philosophy seems to be "get all you can, can all you get, then sit on the can," generosity stands out as a thing of beauty. My aunt Hazel truly found delight in her generous giving. I think it was her spiritual gift! She brought joy to so many around her. Her memory challenges me to this day. Be a giver! Be generous!

Personal Response

On a scale of 1 to 5 (with 1 being *completely unaware* and 5 being *very aware*), how would you rate your awareness of:

- The lonely?   1   2   3   4   5
- The poor?   1   2   3   4   5
- The struggling?   1   2   3   4   5

On a scale of 1 to 5 (with 1 being *I'd rather not* and 5 being *very willing*), how willing are you to share:

- Your words?   1   2   3   4   5
- Your deeds?   1   2   3   4   5
- Your money?   1   2   3   4   5

Prayer

Dear Lord Jesus,

I approach You with a grateful heart. Truly You have blessed me more abundantly than I deserve. I have more than enough of everything, and I thank You. Give me a heart of generosity like Yours. Sensitize me to those in my world who are lonely, poor, or struggling. Impart Your compassion into my heart. I desire that my resemblance to You will be evident, Lord Jesus, as I walk through my daily life. I love You, Lord. Thank You for Your example for me to follow.

Amen.

CHAPTER THREE

THE UNNAMED

Persistent Mother

Then Jesus went out from there and departed to the region of Tyre and Sidon. And behold, a woman of Canaan came from that region and cried out to Him, saying, "Have mercy on me, O Lord, Son of David! My daughter is severely demon-possessed." But He answered her not a word. And His disciples came and urged Him, saying, "Send her away, for she cries out after us." But He answered and said, "I was not sent except to the lost sheep of the house of Israel." Then she came and worshiped Him, saying, "Lord, help me!" But He answered and said, "It is not good to take the children's bread and throw it to the little dogs." And she said, "Yes, Lord, yet even the little dogs eat the crumbs which fall from their masters' table." Then Jesus answered and said to her, "O woman, great is your faith! Let it be to you as you desire." And her daughter was healed from that very hour.

Matthew 15:21–28

A Mother's Plea and Prayer

I had a daughter who was not well.

Her life was controlled by the Prince of Hell.

Her body and mind were so far gone,

Far removed from the days when she was strong.

She was too weak to call for the help she did need,

Too battered and weary to cry out or plead.

How could I help her? What could I do?

It had to be fast; else, she would be "through."

The Healer, Jesus of Nazareth, was coming nearby.

I had to get to Him or give it my best try.

I packed up, got dressed, and started to run!

My only hope was to see God's Son!

I met His disciples, but they turned me away.

Keep going! Find Jesus!

The need was too urgent. I could not delay.

I found Him and knelt before Him twice on my trip,

Pleading for Him to release my daughter from Satan's
grip.

After we conversed for a moment or two,

Jesus sensed my faith and did what *only He could do.*

He healed my daughter, who wasn't even there,

In response to this mother's plea and fervent prayer.

Her Story

This unnamed mother came to Jesus seeking help for her daughter. The girl was *vexed by a demon*, and this left her helpless. No doubt, this mother had explored every other possibility for help near her home. All attempts to rid the child of the demon were futile. When the mother heard the news of Jesus performing impossible feats for others, she was convinced she must get to Him to seek healing for her child. With great anticipation and unswerving faith, she set out to find Him. She was desperate. She needed Jesus!

Learning of Jesus' location, this unnamed mother walked for miles until she arrived in Tyre. When she finally arrived at the house where Jesus was resting, she cried out to Him repeatedly. At first, Jesus did not answer. As a matter of fact, His disciples urged Him to send her away, but this persistent mother was not about to give up. The disciples turned her away several times, but she would not be deterred. Her persistence paid off. Finally, face to face with Jesus, she knelt before Him, worshiped Him, and addressed Him as *Lord* and *Son of David*. She pleaded for her daughter's healing. Jesus granted her request, and her daughter was healed that very hour.

Digging Deeper

The Gospels of Matthew and Mark record the story of the unnamed woman coming to Jesus seeking help for her daughter. From what we can tell, this was a typical day in Jesus' ministry. He had been walking from town to town, teaching crowds of people the ways of His Father and healing the sick who were brought to Him. By the time He arrived on the coasts of Tyre and Sidon, He was exhausted. There, He hoped to withdraw from the crowd and get some much-needed rest. It was in Tyre that this unnamed mother located Him.

Things had not been going well for this mother on her quest to find help for her daughter. She was working against the odds. First, she encountered the disciples who were keeping the crowds away from Jesus so that He could rest. When they saw that she was determined to interrupt Him, they encouraged Him to send her away. Why? She was not one of them—that is, not a Jew. So, they immediately dismissed her and her request. Second, as a Gentile, she was considered a heathen and therefore not worthy of consideration. Historically there was a strong tension between Jews and Gentiles. As a matter of fact, Jews were forbidden to socialize with Gentiles. Third, she was a woman living in a male-dominated culture. There was no mention of her husband, and, in that culture, women had little value without men. It is not surprising that the disciples opposed her. At first, even Jesus appeared to resist her. Yet all these obstacles served only to increase her determination.

When Jesus finally spoke to her, His words were rather shocking. He seemed to dismiss her. He declared that His purpose was to reach the Jewish people. His intent was to show them the will and ways of His Father and instruct the listeners in His pattern for living. Without a doubt, these were not the words this mother expected to hear from Jesus. She knew that, as a non-Jewish person, she did not qualify for a miracle. Still, hoping for His mercy, there was no way that she would allow His words to discourage or deter her.

This mother was on a mission. She had heard of Jesus' previous miraculous healing. She believed that if Jesus could do the impossible for others, He could do the same for her and her daughter despite their religious and ethnic differences. She would persist! There was too much at stake. Once again, she knelt before Him, pleading. She called Him *Lord*. She called Him *Son of David*. These words were not accidental but carefully chosen.

By calling Him *Lord*, she revealed that she recognized Him as *Ruler* or *Master*, the one who was worthy of honor and worship. Her use of the word Lord indicated her willingness to follow Him, that is, to listen to Him and to obey His directives. By addressing Him as *Son of David*, she acknowledged His Jewish identity and His royal heritage. He was a descendant of the noble King David and, possibly, could be the Promised One, the Messiah. This was her declaration of faith!

At her second request for help, Jesus gave an even more shocking response: "It is not good to take the children's bread and throw it to the little dogs" (Matthew 15:26). Initially, this appeared to be an insult from Jesus, but this woman understood what He was saying. His priority was to teach His people, the Jews. Reaching out to a Gentile at this stage of His ministry would be like taking food from God's chosen people and feeding it to dogs. This was definitely a *pushback*, but again, the unnamed mother would not give up. She used Jesus' own analogy to refute His words: "Even little dogs eat the crumbs from the table."

Can you remember when dogs were fed crumbs from the table? We called them "table scraps." In times past, if a dog was fed dry dog food in addition to table scraps, that was a good day for him. Nowadays, there are large refrigerated units in stores filled with various foods strictly for dogs. There are entire department stores dedicated to selling merchandise for pets. Everything from clothing to toys, food, and more. In our land of plenty, how often do pets experience a higher standard of living than many individuals living in other parts of the world, and even here in some parts of the USA? (Just a thought.)

In the Jewish culture at that time, as in ours today, it was not complimentary to refer to a person as a dog. However, in His response, Jesus used the word that related to a little puppy or a house pet, not wild dogs known to rummage through garbage dumps. This mother was not proud. She showed her humility in her response. She would gladly accept the smallest crumb of the Lord's strength and power. Perhaps when this mother met with resistance from the disciples and even Jesus, she might have considered for a brief second that she had dared to cross a cultural barrier. As a Gentile, maybe she appeared too demanding to the

Jewish rabbi. Yet *He* was her only hope. Jesus' reputation preceded Him. *He* was the healer and perhaps the very last possibility for her daughter's deliverance. Therefore, she must persist!

This mother's persistence and confidence pleased Jesus. Her determination and refusal to comply with the disciples' demands touched His heart of compassion. Her *You-are-my-only-answer* faith moved Him to action. He clearly stated that her request was granted. He performed a long-distance healing for her daughter.

How assured, how relieved this mother must have been. Assured, because Jesus declared that due to her faith, her request had been granted. Relieved, because she felt confident in His promise. From that time on, she greatly anticipated returning home to see her daughter delivered. She was not disappointed!

The book of Hebrews tells us: "But without faith it is impossible to please Him, for he who comes to God must believe that He is, and that He is a rewarder of those who diligently seek Him" (Hebrews 11:6).

Although this Scripture verse was not available to this unnamed mother, its truth was lived out in her story. Having heard of Jesus' power, she believed He was from God. She was also convinced that He would reward her faith. He did! After He spoke to her, she was able to rest in the assurance of His words, even though they were spoken from a distance! Sure enough, when the mother returned home, she found her daughter completely well.

We are not told much about the daughter's condition, only that she was vexed or controlled by a demon. We have no indication of exactly how that was manifested in her life. In Matthew, it is stated that she was severely demon-possessed. This indicates she was so tormented by Satan's power that she was unable to seek deliverance in her own strength. All that took place in this story resulted from her mother's observation, compassion, determination, and faith. The daughter never asked for help and yet received healing when she was nowhere near Jesus. This makes me wonder what she thought and how she reacted when the influence of the demon suddenly disappeared. What was it like to relax and not be tormented? Did she experience relief from physical pain? Did a sense of peace wash over her? We don't know.

We are left to wonder how the daughter reacted when her life and body changed completely without even a request on her part. Initially, in her weakened condition, she might not have realized that her mother had gone to seek help. She may not have been aware of who Jesus was, let alone have known of His miraculous power. Yet it was the faith and persistence of her mother that connected her to Jesus. Suddenly, from a distance, the spoken word of Jesus rushed healing power throughout her body, flushing out the power of Satan. I would love to hear her explanation of what happened that day. How was her healing manifested? That's a good question to ponder.

What we *do* know is that Satan no longer had his grip on her.

Oh, how many families have we known through the years who had offspring enslaved by Satan. There are so many addictions and/or negative issues that vie for control of anyone, our youth in particular. Alcohol, sexual misconduct, drugs, pornography, anger, vengeance, dishonesty, greed, hatred, and much more can so grip a person's life that they become dominated by them. Like the daughter, they become so deeply enslaved by the grasp of these deeds or mindsets that they no longer have the strength to reach out for a cure. Often, others look with condemnation on families and/or individuals going through these hardships. However, we know the pull of these evil influences is so varied and so strong that no family is exempt from their grasp.

Jerry and I have known diligent, God-fearing parents who have suffered heartache with one, two, or even three of their children. Often this occurs when the "children" are in their late twenties, thirties, or even forties. That is when they are well past puberty, when maturity, not the dominion of addictions, is expected.

Let us not be judgmental but prayerful and encouraging to those families as they walk through painful days that turn into months and often multiple years. The last thing these people need is condemnation. No, they need a listening ear, a kind word, or any other reminder of our care for them and their family members. These folk need to know that we, their friends, are safe places for them to download their thoughts and feelings. While they are dealing with the depths of these disappointments and hurts, they do not need careless advice or a personal *one-up-you* story. What they need is a trusted listener who will love them and pray for them. They need at least one who will walk with them throughout the entire hardship.

If you know of a family that is presently going through estrangement or the effects of some negative choices, *stop now* and ask the Holy Spirit what you can do to ease their hurt *today*! The smallest gesture of concern might be just the spark of encouragement that gets them through an exceptionally difficult day.

We are not told if this daughter ever expressed appreciation or honor to her mother for all she went through to seek Jesus' help. We do know that the mother left her daily chores, walked what could have been many miles, faced opposition from the disciples, crossed ethnic barriers, and perceived resistance from Jesus. Hopefully, when the daughter was delivered and thinking clearly, she realized her mother's efforts and was grateful for them.

If you are an adult child whose parents are still living, your God-given responsibility is to honor them. Your days of commanded obedience to them are over, but the instruction to honor father and mother lasts as long as the parents live. Honor should spring from a heart of gratitude for the endless care and sacrifices your parents extended during your formative years. However, in our fast-paced world, those deeds often go unrecognized. While there has never been a perfect parent, most (not all) give endlessly to provide for their dependent children.

This could have been through years of work either at home or in the marketplace. Later in life, parents are honored by the appreciation expressed by their children.

What does it mean to honor your parents (or anyone)? According to the New International Webster's Standard Dictionary, honor is defined as "great respect, a mark of special recognition; reputation, an exalted rank, to esteem or respect; to afford special recognition; to recognize or pay as a due debt." That is Webster's definition, but how do we flesh that out?

First, I believe that in order to show honor, one has to be close enough in proximity or thought to know the person, in this case, the parent. Think about them individually. What words, deeds, or gifts would bring them delight? What would speak respect into their life? As you listen to them talk, you will sense what they value. Elderly people are keenly aware that the world is passing them by. They realize they don't know the latest buzzwords or how to operate the latest gadgets. Memory gets rusty. Frustration ensues. These are areas where the patience and love of offspring convey honor.

There's a certain amount of loneliness that accompanies aging. Despite being busy, when adult children take time to communicate, "You are not forgotten. You are in my thoughts. I will always love you," those words or actions have the power to dispel loneliness and bring about the healing honor that is often needed.

A Personal Reflection

Our daughter-in-law is from a large family. A few years ago, we were privileged to share in a Christmas celebration with her extended family. It was a joyous evening of love and honor. The house was filled with people and food. Because the mother of the family had recent surgery, the father had prepared much of the food. Others contributed dishes, but he had prepared a large assortment of delicious hot foods. Even while he hosted the event, he kept a close eye on his wife. Acknowledging her limited mobility, he ensured that her plate and her cup were replenished with whatever she wished. Precious!

The grandchildren opened their gifts and then played joyfully in a room down the hall. Their delight could be heard all over the house. When it came time for the grandparents to open their gifts, the family gathered around. It was time to honor the parents. The children and in-laws eagerly anticipated the parents opening what they had brought specifically for their mom and dad. Each one had put so much love and thought into their gifts. Mom was given a ceramic piece to add to her collection and a special drink that she enjoys. One person made new curtains for her kitchen. She was delighted. Dad received items specially selected for him: a watch and a new wallet. But the "granddaddy" of all his gifts was a scrapbook. Two of the children had combined their ideas and resources to have a scrapbook made of his days in the Navy. When he saw those pictures that were compiled, the joy of those old memories and friends poured out of his eyes. It was great! We saw honor fleshed out that night. Reflections on that evening still fill my heart with delight.

The ten commandments remind us that we add days to our lives when we honor our parents.

Both of my parents were loyal "children" who honored their parents. Each of them set a great example for me.

Another Personal Reflection

My mother was one of three living sisters. One sister lived out of town. The other had no car, and neither did my grandparents. My mom was the one who lived close by and therefore took the care of her aging parents to heart. For as long as either of them lived, she did all she could to enhance their lives. Among other things, this included visits, calls, transportation, financial assistance, and caregiving. She was rewarded with a life of a bit more than ninety-one years due at least in part to her obedience to honor her parents.

My daddy was the oldest son in a five-sibling family. Much like my maternal grandparents, his parents had little of this world's goods. Being keenly aware of this, he did all he could to be of help and encouragement. Daddy had a small produce business. At the end of each workweek, his mother was allowed to glean anything usable. Resourcefully, she was able to stretch her food budget in a delicious way using Daddy's "scraps."

When my grandfather was elderly (or so I thought back then), my daddy would take him to work with him. I don't know if or what financial arrangement they had. I do realize this gave the two of them priceless time together. It certainly brought my Pawpaw a sense of worth. Isn't that honor?

We can continue to honor our parents even after they pass away. As we verbally relate positive memories of them to others, especially the generations after us, we pass down heritage. In doing so, we honor those who have gone before us and make sure their contributions to our family are not forgotten. Certainly, that is one way to honor our parents posthumously.

I want my grandchildren to have a connection to their great-grandparents on both sides of our family. They had wonderful great-grandparents, as well as other family members who left a godly and patriotic legacy. Although these children never had the privilege of a personal relationship with these individuals, their faith, their character traits, and powerful work ethic all need to be remembered. How that is done is left up to us, the middle generation, to figure out.

Just as the faith and persistence of this unnamed mother are recorded for all time, so should the positive influences of our family members be passed down. I have a corner cabinet built by my grandfather in the late 1940s. The top half consists of three open shelves. On the top shelf, I display pictures of my parents and Jerry's parents, along with pictures of each of us with our siblings taken when we were children. On the middle shelf, I keep pictures of "us," that is, Jerry, me, and our kids in years past. All seven of our grandchildren are pictured as babies on the next shelf.

My goal is to write short stories and make scrapbooks of the extended family members to have on hand when the *grands* come to visit. Through this means, our grands will have an opportunity to appreciate contributions and even funny happenings that occurred in years past.

As we review each character in this story, let's ponder the concepts and personal qualities that can be of value to us as individuals.

The Daughter

We don't know her age. We can assume she was old enough to make some negative choices. Quite possibly, she had put herself in compromising situations that permitted demonic forces to influence her life. Perhaps it was something that seemed innocent enough so that she never thought of being trapped in the snare of the devil. Yet it happened. When our narrative began, she was in so deep that she had no ability to seek her own relief. I've heard this quotation many times: *Sin will always take you farther than you want to go, keep you longer than you want to stay, and cost you more than you want to pay.* How true that is. Therefore, whenever temptation presents itself, it is best to *run from it*, not toward it. Satan is never happy with a small influence; he wants control. Run!

> **Satan is never happy with a small influence; he wants control.**

I wonder just how this girl responded when she realized she was delivered. Did it draw her heart to Jesus? Was she appreciative of her mother's efforts? These questions are left unanswered.

The Mother

The normal response of a mother to her child's problem is concern and a desire for resolution. No matter how young, how old, or how convoluted the circumstances might be, a mother is eternally connected to her child. After all, she shared her body with her child. She went through the painful experience of birthing the child. She took care of his every need during the helpless beginning years and beyond. Regardless of their age, when a child hurts, the mother hurts as well. This mother was inseparable from her daughter. The daughter's pain felt like her own. There was no limit to the measures this mother would take to find help for her child.

This mother had a problem in her family that was beyond her ability to solve. News of Jesus' miraculous power had reached her region. No matter how far she had to walk or how long it took her to get to Him, she was determined to get His help. It was *her* daughter who was vexed by a demon. She walked miles, crossed cultural barriers, and faced opposition but never gave up until she secured a resolution for her daughter's situation. This mother was so inextricably connected to her child that when she asked Jesus to help her daughter, she said, "Help *me*!" Selah.

This mother also exemplified worship and faith. Upon seeing Jesus, she fell at His feet. She called Him *Lord*, acknowledging His deity. No matter how much pushback she got, she viewed Jesus as her *only* hope and did not leave until He gave her a positive response. What an example for you and me! No matter the situation or the length of time our child has been affected by wrong influences, we must *never* give up and *never* stop praying or seeking Jesus.

Jesus

This story gives us a different glimpse of Jesus. We see His humanity in that He was tired and seeking solitude. Yet He was *on a mission*, going from place to place, ministering to and healing many people. The disciples attempted to keep this mother from Him, but what initially appeared to her to be rejection was a test of this mother's faith. Her unwavering faith and dogged persistence touched the heart of Jesus, our compassionate Savior. Once again, He showed His *mercy that endures forever* (Psalm 136). If you haven't read that Psalm in a while, I encourage you to do so. It catalogs how His mercy extends throughout all life's circumstances. It has in the past and will endure forever. Never will His mercy give out! It was His mercy and His amazing healing power that brought a complete turnaround in the life of this little family. No matter the crowd size or the complexity of the individual's circumstances, Jesus is ever-present. He is always merciful. He has time for everyone. His unlimited love, mercy, and power that has extended through the ages are still available for our needs today! Selah!

Personal Response

How can we personalize the truths we considered from this story? Let's look at the qualities portrayed by each character.

Jesus

We saw Him demonstrate these qualities:

- He reached beyond His ethnic boundaries.
- He had compassion for a fractured family.
- He proved His power to do the impossible.

What person or persons outside of your own ethnic group or race can you reach out to with compassion?

_____

_____

_____

There are certainly broken, hurting families all around us. Write the first hurting family name that comes to mind and one idea of encouragement you can show them.

Name: _____

Deed of Kindness:_____

Nothing is impossible with Jesus! Do you view Him as *all*-powerful? ☐ Yes ☐ No ☐ I'm working on it

If you need help, read through the book of Luke. His infinite power is revealed throughout the entire book. Write the date you began to read Luke: _____

The Mother

We saw her demonstrate these qualities:

- She was determined to reach Jesus.
- She would *not* give up.
- Her child's restoration was her *top* priority.

On a scale of 1–5, *how* important to you is the salvation and/or spiritual growth of your children?

1   2   3   4   5

Write one thing you can do to push that number higher.

_____

_____

_____

The Daughter

- She had fallen into a trap.
- She was changed by Jesus' mercy.
- Did she honor her mother or praise Jesus?

This girl had an amazing mother. From what we can tell, she would *not* be stopped from getting Jesus' help. Did the daughter ever show honor and/or appreciation? We are not told.

Do you need to take steps to honor your parents, living or posthumously? What could those steps be?

1. _____
   _____

2. _____
   _____

Even if your parents did not lead you into righteousness, you are still commanded to honor them. You can break that generational lack and begin a godly legacy by bridging the gap between the Lord and your children or grandchildren. List two things you can do to make this happen.

1. _____
   _____

2. _____
   _____

Prayer

Dear Father in heaven,

Thank You for this passage of scripture in which I see Your Son proving to be both man and God. Man, in that He grew weary and sought rest. God, in that He demonstrated His ability to do the impossible: overcome the power of Satan and heal from a distance. Thank You for this mother that showed us faith, worship, and determination. I want to learn from this story. Help me to rely on Your power daily, believing that *nothing* is impossible with You! Help me to be unrelenting in bringing my family members to You. Give me wisdom and discernment in reaching out to my family as well as those beyond. Help me to be persistent in following Your directions to me. I pause to listen for Your instruction as I sit quietly in Your presence.

CHAPTER FOUR

THE UNNAMED

Woman with Curvature of the Spine

Now He was teaching in one of the synagogues on the Sabbath. And behold, there was a woman who had a spirit of infirmity eighteen years, and was bent over and could in no way raise herself up. But when Jesus saw her, He called her to Him and said to her, "Woman, you are loosed from your infirmity." And He laid His hands on her, and immediately she was made straight, and glorified God.

Luke 13:10–13

Woman, You Are Loosed!

For eighteen years, my view was down.

I was all bent over, could only see the ground.

While at the temple, Jesus saw my plight,

Called to me and healed me to stand upright.

What a change that day to my life came.

I stood before Him and praised His name!

If you are burdened with cares and strife,

Bent over double with the hardships of life,

Come to Jesus! His power is the same today.

He will heal you, loose you, and send you on your way

To show proof of His power,

As you share your story,

Stand erect and give Him glory!

Her Story

This unnamed woman arrived at the synagogue (the house of worship) on the Sabbath (the day of worship) for the Jewish people. For eighteen years, she suffered from severe curvature of the spine. Her body was so crippled that she could not stand erect but walked bent over. As she was making her way into the synagogue, she heard Jesus call her. "Come to Me," He said. She immediately obeyed. He touched her and declared that she was free of her infirmity. She stood upright and began praising God.

Digging Deeper

My visual imagery of the scene is that of Jesus entering the building or courtyard, preparing to relate to those present what the Father had told Him. He was, no doubt, intensely anticipating His lesson. His heart and mind were aflame with His intended teaching. Yet, as He walked through the crowd, His attention was captured by the arrival of a woman who was so severely bent over that she could not stand erect. His heart of compassion was drawn to her need. His love and mercy compelled Him to reach out to her.

There are four verbs that show Jesus' reaction to the woman. First, He *saw* her. Yes, her physical condition was obvious, but He also *saw* or sensed the misery she had been experiencing for eighteen years. While others were walking right past her, He discerned her need. His insight into her condition moved Him to further action.

Second, He called her to Himself. *Come to Me.* What words of comfort. He was communicating, "I am here for you. Not only do I see your problem, but I am here to bring you love and a solution. My open arms are extended to you. Yes, you, nameless, infirmed worshiper, I am here for *you*!"

Then Jesus *said* or pronounced her healing. "Woman, you are loosed from your infirmity." He verbally declared her healing. What shocking words these had to have been. She must have thought, *Are You speaking to me? This deformity has been with me for almost two decades, and You say this is the time I am delivered?* Awe, amazement, and wonder probably flashed through her mind.

Before she had time to process what was happening, Jesus *laid His hands* on her. Oh, what a moment! As soon as He touched her, her back was healed. Those crooked vertebrae snapped to attention. Immediately, she was able to stand straight for the first time in eighteen years. Selah!

What a powerful story. This woman, who I shall now and hereafter refer to as *Mrs. Bentover*, was an ordinary person who chose to be in the house of worship on the Sabbath. Since she was bent over double, it could not have been easy for her to "go to church." More than likely, she walked very slowly with a cane, maybe even two. She had to prepare and plan ahead. Possibly she had to build in time for rest stops along the way. As difficult as a walk to church was for her with her progressing back disorder, it would have been impossible for her to ride a mule or horse (if either had been available). To our present-day way of thinking, she had good reason to stay home. Not Mrs. Bentover. It took extreme effort, but she was there. As there is no mention of others paying attention to her, it gives me a reason to think her presence at the synagogue was not out of the ordinary. I conclude she was a regular worshiper. Her desire to learn and worship surpassed her need for personal comfort.

No doubt Mrs. Bentover loved the Lord God and prioritized worship. This practice had taught her some of the advantages of consistent corporate worship. She must have had a high view of God, or else she would have never made the extraordinary effort to be at the synagogue. Her hunger for truth continually drew her back to the worship services. We need to remember there were no Bibles to study at home in those days. Corporate worship provided her only connection to God's ways. It also brought about other advantages such as fellowship with other believers, encouragement through praying, singing, and rejoicing together, and opportunities for service.

Mrs. Bentover lived a life beyond self-focus. How easy it would have been for her to live a life defeated in self-pity. Instead of falling into that trap, she took advantage of going to a synagogue where one could mentor or be mentored. There, lasting friendships could be formed. These and other advantages of worship kept our Mrs. Bentover returning to the house of God despite any discomfort it caused her. Regardless of the hardships she endured, Mrs. Bentover did not give up. Her efforts on this day paid off. This was her day for a miracle!

Much like Mrs. Bentover, there was a dear lady who had a similar problem in a church where Jerry and I served. She was severely stooped over. Using a walker, she was able to extend her back enough to be somewhat mobile. However, to talk with her face-to-face, one had to bend over quite a bit. Even when she sat, it was necessary to stoop very low to make eye contact with her. Being familiar with this situation enables me to imagine some of the inconveniences Mrs. Bentover endured.

When the back is deformed, all of life is difficult. Every movement and detail becomes problematic: maintaining balance, reaching items, carrying items, getting up, lying down, bathing, walking, getting dressed, just everything! Consideration has to be put into every action.

Throughout her years of decline, Mrs. Bentover must have sought relief from any medical professionals available to her. She certainly had offered up many prayers to God. On this day, she was simply being faithful, asking for nothing. She was unpretentiously blending in and being a part of the service. Then Jesus showed up with miraculous power, and her life was completely and forever changed. That speaks volumes about Jesus' view of worship and faithfulness. Selah!

She came in "bent over double" and left standing up straight and tall. Then, our scripture states that she "glorified God." What form that took, we do not know. I think the form of worship we choose depends on our personality type and emotional composition. Some people would drop to their knees sobbing words of gratitude. Others might clap, jump, and shout praises. Perhaps Mrs. Bentover stretched as high as her back and neck would allow, delighting in the vantage point she had not been able to enjoy for years. At last, she could see faces rather than knees or feet. What a moment! It was a joyous time for her and those around her. All those nearby who had seen her healing take place gave glory to God for the miracle she experienced, and they witnessed. (Luke 13:13)

While everyone else was rejoicing, one disgruntled person showed up. The Bible states that he was the ruler of the synagogue. I am not sure if he would have been considered the treasurer, the head deacon, the head elder, or even the pastor in today's church structure. Whatever his position, he let it be known in no uncertain terms that he was in charge in that place: "We have our rules in this church. Regardless of what you have just witnessed, *this is the Sabbath!* Our rules strictly prohibit *any* work, even healing the sick, on this day. Now there are six other days that do not carry this restriction. Jesus could have performed this miracle on any of the other six days, and that would have been fine." (Wow! Can you imagine the arrogance of imposing the rules of man over the Son of God? As shocking as this may seem, it does still happen today.)

Jesus' response was quick and firm: "You hypocrite! You self-righteous bigot! How dare you disdain the healing of this dear woman. I know that all those here in attendance today water their donkey or ox on the Sabbath. That requires some form of work, and that for an animal. Don't you realize this woman, a descendant of Abraham, our founding father, is of more value than an ox or donkey? After all, she had been afflicted with this curvature of the spine for eighteen years!"

The power of the Holy Spirit was on Jesus' words. Immediately His words changed the perspective of *all* listening to Him. *All* were put to shame. That is, they were totally embarrassed by the words and actions of their church leader. *All* then rejoiced at *all* Jesus had done. Rather than following the rules and restrictions of the synagogue leader, they witnessed the power of Jesus demonstrated by this healing. They, too, gave Him glory. *All* of them. (Luke 13:17)

Let's take a closer look at Jesus in this passage. He was a man with a purpose. As the Son of God, He knew His time of ministry was brief. His first plan for the day was to teach in the synagogue. However, when He sensed the need of Mrs. Bentover, His plan completely changed. He zeroed in on her. Others could wait. This person had a long-term disability. To Him, her suffering had lasted long enough.

He said, "Come to Me!" It is impossible to utter those words without feeling compassion. As a matter of fact, those words bring memories of our children and grandchildren learning to walk. We adults were there for them. We knew they would fall, but we held out our arms and lovingly called, "Come to me!" Their little legs were unsteady. They were insecure and unbalanced. We adults were there to pick them up and with open arms to embrace them and affirm their progress. Isn't that a snapshot of how Jesus cares for His children, even our Mrs. Bentover?

Disregarding the political correctness of the day, Jesus got involved in the life of Mrs. Bentover, even on the Sabbath. He saw her need. He called her to Himself. He declared words of hope and healing over her situation. Then He touched her. That touch brought about an immediate miracle. She was able to stand up straight and tall for the first time in eighteen years. Oh yes, she glorified God! Selah.

Now let's take a look at Mrs. Bentover. What traits do we find in her that bring home lessons to us individually?

• **She was a worshiper**

The word *worship* is closely akin to the word *worth*. When we worship, we are ascribing worth to the one deserving of our praise. When we view God as the giver of all we have and all we enjoy, it is natural for praise to well up in our souls. This may be expressed to Him in a church setting or anytime and anywhere. On the day recorded in Scripture, Mrs. Bentover chose to worship in her synagogue. She was in the right place at the right time, and her life was changed forever.

• She was obedient

Without hesitation, when Jesus called to her, she came close enough for Him to touch her. She recognized Jesus' voice. She knew His character. She trusted the truth of His words well enough to obey His call immediately. How many times do you or I hear a directive and, rather than obey right then, we contemplate it. That is, we count the cost. We consider just how safe we feel in taking the step of obedience. In our minds, we know the Lord is holy, all-powerful, and trustworthy, but we are just not ready to FROG (fully rely on God). We try to figure out another way.

Procrastination is disobedience. It comes naturally to me. When I ponder the past (which is not always a good idea), I wonder how different my life would have been *if* I had always responded with immediate obedience to every instruction I received from the Lord. How much would I have learned? How much more could I have impacted the lives of others?

I just say, "Thank you, Mrs. Bentover, for exemplifying swift obedience. I appreciate the reminder in this area of life where I need future improvement. I am thrilled that after two thousand years, your encounter with Jesus is still being used to challenge us and to establish truth today."

• She glorified God

Mrs. Bentover had to have been overjoyed at the time of her healing. Without a doubt, that joy led to giving thanks to Jesus for the miracle He had done. As time passed, she might have had to remind others of who she was. Her appearance had drastically changed. She had to tell them, "Remember me? I am Mrs. Bentover. For eighteen years, I had a horrible curvature of the spine. Look at me now. Because Jesus touched me, I now stand straight. I am pain-free. I can walk and live like others. I know the power of God. I personally experienced Jesus' healing touch that changed my life. Oh, how He deserves credit for all His love, provisions, and miracles He has given to all of us."

At this point, I am wondering how many times have we heard prayers concluded with, "...and we'll be sure to give You the praise and the glory for what You do..."? I have heard that hundreds of times, but do we keep that promise? He is deserving of our awe! He is deserving of our praise, regardless of how quickly or how long it takes for the answers to our prayers to arrive.

Mrs. Bentover exemplified worship, obedience, and glorifying God. Pause to consider how you are learning and growing in these areas. Selah.

By reading through this account, we can conclude there were quite a few onlookers. Perhaps many of them had been acquainted with Mrs. Bentover over the years. They had witnessed her condition worsen as time passed. Maybe they felt some pity for her, but on this day, none of them reached out to her with love or concern. We conclude that each of them had their own priorities. Maybe they had grown to accept her condition as normal or even hopeless. So why bother to offer assistance or a word of encouragement? Their thinking may have been: *That's just her lot in life. I can't do anything about it.*

Do we project this same attitude? Are we so consumed with our own schedules—our priorities—that we are too busy to sense a need? Do we accept the discouraged, the lonely, the hurting, as hopeless the way they are? Like these churchgoers, do we also think there's nothing we can do about that problem? Not true! Even the simplest deed of care can bring the sunlight of God's love into a person's day.

How many people does it take to change an attitude or a situation? I would say just one! Because both Jerry and I are heart patients, this past year of COVID-19 has been quite a challenge. The uncertainty of it all has caused us to be at home for more months than we initially anticipated. We live in a good neighborhood surrounded by nice people. Often some would say, "Let me know if you need anything." I appreciate that statement and truly believe any one of them would willingly pick up our medications or any needed groceries. However, there was one lady who took things into her own hands. She would call or drop by, stating she was going out. She then offered to pick up items for us. On numerous occasions, she shopped for us, even in the rain. With our list and debit card in hand, she joyfully met our needs. I ask you, which person made the difference? Which *one* made this neighborhood seem like a caring place? The one who made herself available. The one willing to get involved.

How many individuals does it take to make an outsider feel welcome at church? After Jerry and I retired, we started looking for a church home. We visited quite a few churches. There were some where people knew us from our past and others where we were total strangers. We sincerely wanted to find a place close by where there was acceptance as well as meaningful teaching. Excuse me while I chase a "furry little rabbit."

We visited a church nearby that looked like a possibility. I was elated that one lady came and talked to me with warmth and kindness. Others spoke to us as well, but she was the one who made me feel welcomed. So, we visited again. I saw this lady, and I feel confident she saw us, but she never made any effort to speak to us on our second visit. What a disappointment! Could her acceptance on the second visit have made a difference in our decision? We will never know.

Until recently, many churches included a "meet and greet" segment in their services. I think that is a good thing. An obligatory *hello* is better than nothing. However, it takes much more than that to make an outsider feel accepted and valued. It takes *one*, maybe *two*, who engage in conversation and express concern. The question is this: Do we really want newcomers in our community or those seeking truth in our church? If the answer is *yes*, those established in the church or neighborhood *must* reach out. Notice unfamiliar faces. Make an effort to speak to those you don't know. Make conversation—not just, "Hello, glad to see you." Ask for their name and any interest they may have in church or community activities. Invite them to sit with you (even if you have to move away from your regular seating). Pray for them or with them. Look for them to return and continue to express interest in their lives. Invite them to lunch. Become a friend. After all, a stranger is a friend you haven't met yet.

> ### *A stranger is a friend you haven't met yet.*

Through these and other simple acts, *all* of us can make a difference in the life of an outsider, and that outsider could become a valued, lifelong friend. Our simple acts of kindness could mean their salvation and spiritual growth. As one individual, you or I can make a difference in the expansion of our church's influence or the atmosphere in our family or neighborhood.

A Personal Story

Our daughter is married to an Air Force officer. They have had to move numerous times. One of the most difficult challenges they face is "being new" over and over again. In some places, they have found delightful church settings and welcoming neighborhoods. In other places, they have gone three years or more with the entire family never feeling they belonged in a fellowship of believers or the community around them. That is painful! How different their lives would have been in either of these settings if only one, two, or three individuals had shown sincere interest.

Being "settled in" can be a hindrance to inclusion. How easy it is for those who have lived in the same place and gone to the same church for years to be comfortable and not realize how it feels to be "on the outside looking in." It is not comfortable being in a new setting. It is awkward to be in a place where you don't know anyone around you, plus you are totally unfamiliar with the surroundings. When just one or two individuals sense this and reach out warmly, it eases the tension and makes the place seem welcoming.

Another Personal Story

Recognizing outsiders is much more difficult in a large church setting than in a small one. However, I know for sure it is possible. When Jerry and I were on vacation in Branson, Missouri, we visited a very large church. What an awesome experience! We were welcomed warmly in the visitors' parking lot and then directed to the front door. We were welcomed by a greeter there and given further directions. The usher at the entrance to the sanctuary escorted us (as at a wedding) to our seats of choice. There we were greeted by those seated nearby. After the service, several individuals greeted us and introduced us to their friends. When we left, we received the same welcoming treatment in reverse, all the way back to our car. You better believe both Jerry and I anticipate being able to visit and worship in that church again. It was unbelievable!

My "furry little rabbit" grew into a larger one, huh? Hopefully, you get the point. People need acceptance. All people need to feel love expressed. There are tiny acts of courtesy that all of us can do to make others feel valued. These tiny deeds can be the inroad to a new life for them not only in the church but in our community, workplace, and family as well. These often-unseen acts of kindness can be bridges to new relationships. They can be the "mortar that matters" to bring warmth and acceptance to a person in need.

Often, we are reluctant to get involved in the lives of others. Doing so could become time-consuming. It might cost more than we want to pay. Aren't you glad that Jesus doesn't make excuses but gets involved in our lives? Sometimes He sends individuals to get involved in our life who influence our major decision-making. During my high school days, I babysat for a family in my home church. They saw potential in me. They reached out to me in ways that determined where I went to college, which ultimately determined whom I married. I'd say their care greatly impacted my life! It has been many years, and I still keep in touch with them. I'll be eternally thankful that they got involved in a way that set the future trajectory of my life.

Fast forward many years. During a time of uncertainty, a friend challenged me to apply for employment at the local school board. I did, and that involvement is benefiting our lives through the present. Because we moved around a bit and I had taught in Christian schools in previous years, I thought I would never have any retirement benefits, but I do. Just my insurance plan is quite a blessing to us during retirement. This resulted from *one* friend who took the time to listen and get involved when my life was at a crossroads.

There are others who have been there at pivotal times in my life. They are a godsend! No doubt there are people you can recall who have been game-changers for you. They were there for you during times of uncertainty or confusion. If possible, give them a call. Let them know how much their care impacted your life. Then, as you go about your everyday life, make yourself available to be a game-changer for someone else. I believe these encounters occur in the natural flow of life. They usually are not planned. They occur as we are open to the leadership of the Holy Spirit.

Wouldn't you like to have input into the lives of others, input that provides godly guidance? I would. Let us pray to that end. The smallest deed, suggestion, or conversation could be the *mortar* that *matters* to bring help or direction that has a lifelong bearing on another person. Be like Jesus. Be available. Be flexible. Reach out to others every time He opens a door. Jesus was there for Mrs. Bentover that day. His involvement changed her life from that moment on.

Personal Response

On a scale of 1 to 5 (1 indicating the need for great improvement and 5 indicating that you're doing okay), rate yourself on concepts from this chapter.

- Like Jesus, my schedule is flexible enough to be interrupted to care for hurting people.

  1   2   3   4   5

- I am likely to be the one person who makes my community or church a welcoming place for others.

  1   2   3   4   5

- I obey immediately when given a directive by the Lord.

  1   2   3   4   5

- My worship is a lifestyle, not one hour per week.

  1   2   3   4   5

- Friends and others feel safe coming to me with their cares.

  1   2   3   4   5

- I desire to be a game-changing influence on those around me.

  1   2   3   4   5

Evaluate your responses. Ask the Lord to show you specific ways to experience improvement in the areas that indicate a lack.

Prayer

Dear Lord Jesus,

I am thankful for this brief passage of Scripture. Thank You for the insights I gleaned from Your example. Now I see my need for personal growth in the areas of worship, obedience, outreach, and flexibility. Show me how to use my time to honor You as well as to be sensitive to the needs of those around me. As I sit here quietly before You, I ask for Your wisdom in following Your example of compassion.

Afterword

Some thoughts on worship.

When I was a child, my concept of worship was "going to church services to learn from the Bible." That meant setting aside Sunday as a day devoted to God and to rest. Services at my home church included age-appropriate classes for children and nursery care for babies. In the adult services, there was always joyful music, Bible reading, several prayers, offerings given, plus an opportunity to respond and pray at the conclusion. Frequently there were testimony times, usually in the evening service. Anyone who wanted to express praise to God was allowed to speak. These were great times of insight and inspiration to me as a child as I heard adults tell of God's hand in their lives during the previous week. Some would tell of the Lord's protection. Another might express a new insight into a scripture. Others might list items of thanksgiving. I knew these adults well. As I heard them talk, they made a powerful and positive impact on my young heart and mind.

At these services, we learned to live beyond ourselves. We also learned to reach out and bring others in. Foreign missionaries played an important part in our church experience. Costumed missionaries from around the globe came and shared their work through pictures, spoken word, and artifacts. Sometimes it was scary, but always interesting. Powerful evangelists came in as well as excellent musicians. Ensembles and choirs came in from Christian colleges. As a teen, I was most privileged to experience a true revival. This was not just a week of special meetings. It was a time when the Holy Spirit showed up profoundly. Services lasted far past the intended time as people prayed at the altar. These services were extended past the week allotted, and they were awesome in the truest sense of the word.

I was unusually blessed to have had all these experiences. I guess all the above-stated reasons are why I find it difficult to accept that the word "worship" in recent years has been relegated to singing. I absolutely love Christian music. My mom played Christian radio in our home as I was growing up. She often went about her daily chores singing. My parents provided piano lessons for my sister and me (with the intended result of our being able to play in church). I've been married to a singer for more than half a century. His family sang in many churches in North

Carolina and Virginia as he was growing up. He sang in various groups in college. In the Navy, he sang his way through boot camp in the Blue Jacket Choir. He served as a music director for twenty-one years and directed all the music in another twenty years of pastoral ministry. We *love* music. However, worship is far more than singing. I have come to the conclusion that worship is a way of life.

There is not much I can do to change the present perception that music is worship. However, I can be a worshiper all day, every day. As I discipline my thoughts through the reading of the Word, talking to the Lord about everything, and continually giving thanks for *every* blessing I can think of, I grow in worship. We have so many resources available to us today that can enhance our worship. We have godly radio broadcasting and numerous Christian television stations (for me, absolute godsends during COVID-19). Study-helps and books galore are all around us. So far, we still have church ministries open to us. We certainly have a new appreciation for all these since the pandemic, right? Cultivating godly friendships is a precious essential. We need those in our lives with whom we can discuss biblical issues and pray. It certainly enriches our lives to have deep friendships, more than just eating-out buddies. These and other factors keep our minds "stayed on Him," that is, in an attitude of worship.

Excuse me while I chase another little rabbit. Several years ago, I attended a sizable ladies' retreat. During the breaks, the ladies' rooms had waiting lines. Of course, there was lots of chatter. I will never forget what one enthusiastic woman said. Using hand gestures, she demonstrated how a cup filled with liquid would spill over into the saucer when moved from one place to another. Her analogy was this: We, too, should be so filled with the truth and goodness of God that we spill into the lives of others as we go about our everyday tasks. When we are filled, we spill! That is, as we become continual worshipers, it is natural for us to overflow onto others. Aren't we left here for that purpose? Oh yes, we sing, but growing in our worship involves far more than just singing.

After we practice some or all of the disciplines mentioned above, we can go to the house of worship so filled with insights, gratitude, and answers to prayer that we spill over into the lives of others. After all, *when we're filled, we spill*!

When we are filled, we spill.

We, worshipers, go to service with the desire to *be* a blessing as well as to *receive* a blessing. One way we can be a blessing is to arrive early. Look around for someone sitting or standing alone. Your care and conversation might be just what they need to get past a rough spot on their road of life. When we are used to bring encouragement to another, we receive the "splash-back" as well. That is, we are inspired or encouraged as much or more than the other person. Both of us then light a spark of worship. We go into the service to sing, pray, study, and take notes. We can keep the flame of worship burning as we make connections and share notes with that person after the service. Compare what each of you was challenged to be or do in the days that follow. Maintain contact and accountability, which could lead to a growing friendship. Worship then becomes a learning, growing, exciting experience for both persons involved. Singing is a delightful part but far from all that is included in worship.

CHAPTER FIVE

THE UNNAMED

Widow of Nain

Now it happened, the day after, that He went into a city called Nain; and many of His disciples went with Him, and a large crowd. And when He came near the gate of the city, behold, a dead man was being carried out, the only son of his mother; and she was a widow. And a large crowd from the city was with her. When the Lord saw her, He had compassion on her and said to her, "Do not weep." Then He came and touched the open coffin, and those who carried him stood still, and He said, "Young man, I say to you, arise." So he who was dead sat up and began to speak. And He presented him to his mother. Then fear came upon all, and they glorified God, saying, "A great prophet has risen up among us"; and, "God has visited His people." And this report about Him went throughout all Judea and all the surrounding regions.

Luke 7:11–17

The Widow of Nain

I lived in a small town called Nain,
A "nowhere" place until Jesus came.
Widowed, grieved, and totally heartbroken,
I had no hope before His words were spoken.
"Do not weep," He said to me.
What did He mean? How could this be?
Stepping into my life of deepest despair
When pain and sorrow were more than I could bear.
Yes, Jesus came and did what others dared not do.
He touched a coffin and spoke to the dead, too.
No human could resist His voice.
When He said, "Arise," my son had no choice.
Up from the dead, he came that day.
Amazed and elated, what could I say?
The crowd went crazy, as well they would,
As Jesus restored my family when no one else could.

Her Story

When we meet this unnamed woman, we know from the information given that she is widowed. Without a doubt, she had already been through immeasurable grief and loss. As Jesus and His followers arrive in her hometown of Nain, she and her family and friends are on their way to bury her only son, who had died. Apparently, he was a young man, single and living at home with his mother. The heartache she was experiencing was almost more than she could bear. This present day was devastating. Yet without her husband and only son, her future looked worse. The world that she had known had collapsed. It was too late for hope and too late for help...or so she thought.

Digging Deeper

I love the Gospel of Luke. It chronicles the life of Jesus, going about *just being Jesus*. Prior to this passage, He had given the Sermon on the Mount, which was radical teaching for that time. (But that is a completely different study.) Then in Capernaum, He healed the centurion's servant in response to the commander's humility and faith. Everywhere He went, He was showing mercy and love to crowds and individuals while doing the impossible. He was *just being Jesus*.

In this story, Jesus entered the city of Nain with a large crowd of His followers when He saw a funeral procession accompanied by many mourners. It was not like the funeral processions of today, with a hearse followed by

111

a long line of slowly moving cars, often preceded by a police escort. These people were traveling by foot, with the coffin being borne on the shoulders of several men, probably the deceased's family members or friends.

This was the funeral procession of a young man, the only son of a widowed mother. Her grief was unbearable. Not only had her husband died, but now her son had died as well. This was the worst possible day of her life. Her future looked dark and hopeless.

Interestingly, while writing this chapter, we received a newsletter from Jentezen Franklin's ministry. In referencing the widow of Nain, he pointed out that at that place and time, women were not property owners. When a woman was widowed, any family property and assets were passed to the oldest son. He then was responsible for the care of his widowed mother. If there was no son to receive this responsibility, the estate was passed on to another family member or even a stranger who might not have the widow's interest at heart. This could leave a widow living as a homeless beggar.

Into this scene of loss and sorrow, Jesus came. His immediate focus was on one unnamed, heartbroken mother. First, the passage stated that Jesus *saw* her. I believe this means much more than His ability to see her with His physical eyes. Yes, He saw her (probably dressed in funeral garb and overcome by sorrow). On a deeper level, He *saw* her devastation, her grief, her broken heart. He knew she had already mourned the loss of her husband.

Now, she was witnessing the impending burial of her only son. Yet, Jesus planned His day to be there at her point of deepest distress. Oh, that is so characteristic of His going about *just being Jesus*.

He stopped to talk to her, but what He said to her humanly made no sense. He said, "Do not weep." Really? She was probably thinking, *Of course I'm weeping. I've lost my husband, and now my son has died. My world has crashed. My hope for the future is gone. I'm grasping at the fact that the life of my only child has been snuffed out way too prematurely. How can You say, "Do not weep"?*

Rather than responding to those thoughts, Jesus went about *just being Jesus*! He got involved with the crisis at hand. He went into the funeral procession and did something not politically correct for that time and religious setting. He touched the open coffin and possibly the corpse. Touching a corpse was a violation of the law handed down by Moses, and the mourners would be aware of this. Certainly, those present were watching Jesus closely and were totally confounded by His involvement with the dead.

I would dare to guess that the funeral procession stopped at that point! However, Jesus was not finished working in this situation. He got even more radically involved. He talked to the dead! Really! By this time, I am positive all eyes and ears were on Jesus. *What is He doing? What is He saying?*

Jesus addressed the deceased directly: "Young man, I say to you, arise." Before the people could register fear or disbelief, the dead person responded. Without hesitation, the young man sat up. What a shocker that had to have been for the people in the crowd. Then the man spoke.

Dead people do not sit up. Dead people do not talk. Jesus had done it again. As He was going about *just being Jesus*, He had done the impossible. He showed both His compassion and His power. Miracle of all miracles, He had raised the dead to life. Selah!

Can you imagine the reactions of the bystanders? Shock, joy, disbelief, fear, and who knows what else? What a day to be following Jesus! What a day to be in Nain! Wahoo!

The next sentence in the narrative is: *And He presented him to his mother.* Family restoration! What an exciting part of this story. What Jesus was communicating to the unnamed widow was that He was doing this for her. He was healing her grief-stricken heart. He was returning her son to her alive, well, and transformed by the power of God. Selah!

Without a doubt, the people in the crowd that day were left with their jaws dropping. They had never seen anything like this, yet they realized the source. Certainly, this was the work of God's hand. No ordinary man could raise the dead. The passage declares that *all* there gave glory to God, stating: *God has visited His people.*

No doubters. No naysayers. Everyone who witnessed the miracle gave honor to the Lord. What a time of unity and worship. What a day to be at the graveyard near Nain. The strong presence of God had to be overpowering, totally unforgettable. Oh, that our response to His goodness and compassion to us was that of total praise. Oh, that we would honor Him for every evidence of His power we witness continually. Selah!

Verse 17 makes me chuckle: "And this report about Him went throughout all Judea and all the surrounding regions." You bet! With news as exciting as this, we can feel sure word spread rapidly: "Did you hear about Jesus raising Mrs. So-and-so's son from the dead? Hey, I was there. He really was dead. No doubt about it. We were heading to the cemetery, and then Jesus came. You would not believe what Jesus did and how quickly the boy revived!"

Combine the small-town crowd gathered to show support and to attend the funeral with the crowd that was following Jesus; quite a few people witnessed this miracle that put Nain on the map. In spite of being limited only to word of mouth, we can be assured that this news spread like wildfire throughout the region, as what could have been a couple of hundred people or many more (maybe even thousands) went about recounting the events of that day to others.

This is the only mention of Nain in the entire Bible. I checked the concordance. I looked for its location in my Bible maps. Not to be found. (I have seen it on one map since I began this writing.) That leads me to believe this was an extremely small town. Perhaps so small that it could be considered what an evangelist friend called a *poke and plumb* town, meaning by the time you poked your head out the car window to take a look around, you would be plumb out of the little town. We've all been to tiny places like that.

Maybe you live in a place so tiny that it doesn't make it on a map, big or small. Consequently, you may feel unimportant to others and even to the Lord Jesus. Not so. Jesus showed us through this passage that He is aware of places that have no claim to fame, nor do the residents have any notoriety.

No place is too insignificant for Him to come and show His mercy. No time is inconvenient for Him to show up to do the impossible. No task is insurmountable for His power. No person is insignificant in the eyes of Jesus. Here in Nain, on this day, He came to an unnamed mother and her unnamed son in a nowhere place. Unannounced, *just being Jesus*, He came and miraculously changed their family dynamic. Selah!

Family units are God's plan for mankind. Home should be a place of peace and refuge for us all. Of course, that is not always the case. Family problems and divisions are prevalent. Often, hurt is not only around us but deep within us. Humanly speaking, circumstances may seem impossible to resolve.

Recently I heard Christine Caine say, "Impossible is where God starts. Miracles are what God does." What a comfort! Are you involved in a family issue that is impossible in your eyes? I am. There is no human resolution to the situation. I get it. Been there and going through another episode. I *cannot* fix it. Much like the unnamed mother in our story, unless Jesus steps in, it is hopeless.

Yet, Jesus did step into her life when the need was the greatest. As He was going about *just being Jesus*, He brought family restoration. *He presented the son to his mother.* When all hope was gone, death was present; Jesus restored life and family! Selah! Selah again!

Isn't the Word of God amazing? Just seven short verses, Luke 7:11–17, explode with truth. Jesus' visit to Nain spanned only a part of one day. Yet it gives us a snapshot of the lives He touched in miraculous ways as He went about *just being Jesus*.

We know He reached out to a grieving mother, raised the dead, and restored her family. Let's take a closer look at those present in Nain that day and consider what they may have experienced.

The Mother

We know very little about her, not even her name. The facts that are given only speak of death, sorrow, and hopelessness. Her family of three had been reduced to one. With the deaths of her husband and only son, she was alone. Life then seemed like a dead-end street, the end of her family and her future. Then even without her request, Jesus arrived.

When He instructed her not to weep, He was not being

crass or dismissive. He understood her tears. There is a difference between crying and weeping. I am a crier. I cry when I'm happy, when I'm sad, when I'm blessed, and when little children sing about Jesus. That is my emotional response. However, weeping takes on another whole dimension. Weeping is a gut-wrenching, uncontrollable response to a situation totally out of one's control. That is where this mother was when Jesus arrived. He saw, and He cared! His mere presence demonstrated compassion. As He took command of the situation, this dear mother witnessed both His love and His power. His power over death certainly took her from tears of sorrow to tears of joy. As Jesus tenderly presented him (her son, alive and well) to his mother, she experienced Jesus' love deeply and personally.

Within a short time, her emotions went from total devastation to indescribable joy, all because Jesus stepped into her life *just being Jesus*. Although she never asked for a thing that day, she was on the receiving end of His compassion, power, and love. Selah!

The Son

This young man was definitely on the receiving end of God's goodness that day in Nain. As the narrative began, he was unquestionably stone-cold dead. He had *no* ability to ask anything of Jesus. Then on the way to his own burial, the Master spoke to him. With one command, "Young man, I say to you, arise." he sat up and spoke. The very first image he saw was the loving face of Jesus.

Selah! Jesus then extended His hand to present him to his mother, alive and strong. What power He demonstrated as He went about *just being Jesus*!

In what were probably seconds, the young man was transformed from the cold grip of death to a moving, talking individual, walking with his hand clasped in the hand of Jesus. Wouldn't you love to hear his account of that day? I would.

The Crowd

We have no way of knowing how many onlookers viewed the miracle at Nain. The Bible clearly states there was a crowd of folk who came to mourn with the mother and to give her emotional support. To that number, whatever it was, Jesus brought another crowd of followers. Each one of them was a receiver that day. These people were in the right place at the right time to witness the power of God. Any doubt in Jesus they may have had upon arrival was wiped away by what they saw. Any unbelief was replaced with joy and worship. They were in the presence of the Son of God. They all saw Him do the impossible. *All* recognized this was the power of God. *All* glorified Him! (Luke 7:16)

Jesus' power and His compassion have not diminished at all. Today, He is fully aware of everything facing all people. He has immeasurable compassion for His children and power to change *any* and *all* circumstances. So, let's give our mess to Him and expect to see His power work in our families, this day, this month, this year. He is able! Selah.

In this story, we saw Jesus *just being Jesus*. He saw. He spoke. He touched. That is His pattern for us: be aware, declare, be there.

> ## *That is His pattern for us: be aware, declare, be there.*

As you and I go about our daily lives, we too should see; *be aware*. That is, we should observe the situations others are experiencing. With the help of the Spirit, we can become sensitive to pain, tears, and isolation. After assessing the problem, Jesus spoke to the mother and to the son. Sometimes we need to be silent when someone is hurting. Other times we need to *declare* our concern and God's truth in a situation. Also, Jesus was there. He changed His schedule and went out of His way to *be there* for this unnamed mother and son!

When we are aware of others with a personal crisis, we, too, need to *be there* for them. Sometimes that takes the form of what I call the *ministry of presence*, just being with the hurting person. When someone is in the depths of hurt or sorrow, they need to know there is at least one individual who cares enough to be in the room with them and just sit with them. Words may not be necessary. Being present to support and listen is the immediate need. This can be followed up by other gestures of concern, but it is the *being there* that initially is of greatest value.

Excuse me while I chase another *furry little rabbit*.

About ten years ago, Jerry and I were experiencing personal devastation. It was a time of deep hurt, rejection, and uncertainty. Although our sister-in-law lived two thousand miles away, her heart was extended to us in such a meaningful way that I took notes on her phone call. She called. She spoke softly. She listened. She did *not* interject similar problems of others. She expressed her concern and assured us of her prayers. Now, that is the way to be there in time of need. Although she was far away, she definitely demonstrated the *ministry of presence*. From across the country, she listened!

Listening is a cultivated art. While it is something we are all capable of, we need to be intentional. It is natural for us to talk about ourselves and/or our families and friends when it is listening that is needed. Having one person who cares enough to *hear the hurt* goes a long way in easing emotional pain. Listening requires self-discipline and practice. As difficult as that may be, it will supply opportunities to touch the lives of others deeply. Selah!

Think about listening. Is that an area in your life that needs conscious honing? Have you given thought to your need to be a listener or your need to have a listener? Any time you go through a crisis, you will sense its importance.

Here are some thoughts I wrote down from that sensitive contact from my sister-in-law. It took place a decade ago, yet it still affects my response to others.

- Listen to what is said and what is not said. Listen for pain.

- If words are necessary, speak tenderly.

- When in-person, maintain eye contact.

- Hear the hurting person out. Do not interrupt.

- Do not tell stories of others in similar situations (unless urged by the Holy Spirit). Realize the hurting person is experiencing all the emotional load they can carry. Their issue is all-consuming at the moment.

- Leave the conversation with the assurance of your continued concern and prayers.

- Give the person some time, then follow up with another contact expressing your care.

There are people all around us who are hurting. Often, conscientious or quiet people will not ask for help. They don't want to be a bother. They may even feel it is their fate to endure hardship. Unless we build a bridge of trust between them and ourselves, we can walk right past them and never realize that internally they are crying out in pain.

Bridge-building is our job. We need to be building relationships with others continually. Selflessness and intentionality are necessary. This could mean listening when you are bone tired. It could mean going an inconvenient *second mile*. It could mean staying up late and making something meaningful for a specific person. It could mean sharing items that you intended for yourself. It could mean so much more. Bridge-building must always include prayer. It is only as the Holy Spirit of God touches and empowers our efforts that they truly meet the need of the hurting.

Jesus was with a crowd, and He also walked into a crowd. But it was *one* individual, one unnamed, grieving mother He ministered to that day. He could have chosen to weep with her and pray for her and then go on His way. He didn't! He zeroed in on *one* woman and stayed with her until her life's trajectory was completely changed. He was *just being Jesus*!

You and I are not Jesus, but we are His followers. Therefore, we should resemble Him in our words and deeds. We can follow His example as we move through life with me just being *me* and you just being *you*. Whoever you are (Pam, Joann, Judy, Kathy, Norma, Chris), determine to walk in Jesus' footsteps as you seek to *be aware, declare, and be there* for those you are entrusted to impact daily.

Will you accept the challenge of reaching out to *one* person per day? That could mean as many as 365 touches for the year. So, you miss a few. Even 300 or 200 would make a tremendous difference in your world, the world of others, and ultimately the *whole world*! How this would look is as varied as we are individuals. You know what you can do and what you can't do. Just be yourself, using the skills and abilities God has given you to bless other people, especially the sick, the lonely, and the hurting.

Set a goal. Reach out to one person every day.

Okay, let's get started. Ask the Lord, right *now*, what person in your sphere of influence you should give a spark of cheer today. On your calendar, mark the names of those you reach out to day by day. Keep up with those you touch. Go back and follow up. Before long, reaching out to others will become a joyful way of life. Good start. Now only 299 or 199 left to go this year (depending on your goal).

I must tell you the story of the purple mums:

Quite a few years ago, I bought a little six-pack of bedding plants. It cost maybe a few cents more than a dollar. There were six plants with a shade of purple/lavender bloom that was very appealing to me. I always thought mums were annual (one year only) autumn (one season only) plants. Boy, did I get a surprise!

During year one, I planted the mums between some bushes close to our front wall. They bloomed and were very pretty. The next year they came up again. Oh, was I ever shocked and pleased! Once again, they bloomed until frost. By the third year, I came to the realization they needed more sun, so I replanted them into our front island in full sun. Oh my, they went ballistic!

Clasp your hands and extend them from your body as far as you can. Each one grew that big. They were loaded with blossoms that kept recurring as long as I deadheaded them. That little one-dollar investment brought me tons of joy. Each year they spread more and more. I have shared some plants with a neighbor, a friend in a neighboring town, a friend in South Carolina, and my daughter-in-law in North Carolina. Are you getting the picture of potential? The little mums have spread into two neighborhoods and two more states. Also, they have dropped thousands of seed pods. Who knows how many plants or blooms they could potentially produce?

So it is with our outreach seeds. Yes, the first intended person is blessed. How that will grow and multiply, we have *no* way of knowing. Take the challenge. Reach out to someone in your own unique way every day possible. Scatter seeds of help, love, compassion, and thoughtfulness as you go about *just being you.* Only God knows how far that influence will reach.

In recounting the events of that day in Nain, I feel sure *all* the people present continued to give glory to God for weeks, months, years, and probably for the rest of their lives. They were the individuals that "spread this report throughout all Judea and all the surrounding regions." *Just being themselves* (Benjamin, Eli, Martha, Aaron,

Mary, Sarah, Nathan) were left to spread the message of this miracle to others in their sphere of influence. Isn't that our purpose in life? As we go about our daily lives *just being ourselves*, shouldn't we be blessing others and pointing them to the transforming power of Jesus?

_____

_____

Personal Response

1. List the first three individuals that come to mind who could use your encouragement today.

_____

_____

_____

2. What is one way you could build a bridge to them?

_____

_____

_____

3. What are two skills or abilities you have and could use to build that bridge?

_____

_____

_____

4. What name comes to mind when you think of a hurting family?

   _____

   _____

   _____

5. What is one way you could reach out with comfort to them today?

   _____

   _____

   _____

Prayer

Dear Father in heaven,

I thank You for Your Word. I thank You for opening my mind to this tiny passage. Let me not forget the concepts before me. I do desire to grow in the likeness of Your Son, Jesus. Please show me the individuals I can love and encourage. Give me ideas and methods to reach them. Show me how to use skills and abilities I already possess to bring a spark of Your love into their lives.

Use me to spread the mortar of love between the bricks of their brokenness to build a wall of faith in You. Amen.

Afterword

There are three chapters in this book that give us insights into the life of the widowed. Now, as in Bible times, widows face hardships and many changes. In James 1:27, we are reminded of our responsibility to offer comfort and assistance to those making vast adjustments to life without their spouse: "Pure and undefiled religion before God and the Father is this: to visit orphans and widows in their trouble, and to keep oneself unspotted from the world."

Before the pandemic struck, our initial response to the widowed was positive. When someone lost a spouse, family members and friends reached out with visits, food, cards, and flowers. Warm embraces were in abundance. Each of these expressions of love was greatly appreciated, often leaving warm memories for a lifetime. But what about two months, six months, or a year later? That is when the finality of the situation sets in, and the widowed feels "half" and not fitting in anywhere. These are the days and the evenings when a simple phone call with a listening ear is needed. Any expression of care could bring incredible encouragement. "You are not forgotten" can be expressed in many ways: a card, an invitation, and inclusion into your world in varied ways.

My mother-in-law expressed to me how helpful her church family was during our Papaw's illness. Then, when he passed, the helpers disappeared. Just when she needed minor repairs or advice for the same, no one was available.

My point is: as important as the initial remembrance is, it needs to continue endlessly.

Recently I was talking with my oldest remaining cousin, late eighties. She lives alone and has some physical limitations. I could literally "hear her smile" as she related to me over the phone what godsends her neighbors are to her. Every time they make soup, chili, or anything shareable, they bring her enough for two days. Each day, they bring her mail from the street to her door. They notice minor repairs that are needed and take care of them unsolicited. She was praising God for their kindness to her.

How does that relate to you and me? Stop and think, *What widowed person do I know that needs my kindness* today? *Who needs a phone call? Who would be encouraged to receive a pretty notecard expressing loving thoughts? Who would be overjoyed by a drop-in visit, a flower from my yard, or a banana bread?*

Yes, we need to express our love to the widowed initially, but six months, a year, two or three later, the need is even greater. Selah!

CHAPTER SIX

THE UNNAMED

Woman with the Issue of Blood

Now a certain woman had a flow of blood for twelve years, and had suffered many things from many physicians. She had spent all that she had and was no better, but rather grew worse. When she heard about Jesus, she came behind Him in the crowd and touched His garment. For she said, "If only I may touch His clothes, I shall be made well." Immediately the fountain of her blood was dried up, and she felt in her body that she was healed of the affliction. And Jesus, immediately knowing in Himself that power had gone out of Him, turned around in the crowd and said, "Who touched My clothes?" But His disciples said to Him, "You see the multitude thronging You, and You say, 'Who touched Me?'" And He looked around to see her who had done this thing. But the woman, fearing and trembling, knowing what had happened to her, came and fell down before Him and told Him the whole truth. And He said to her, "Daughter, your faith has made you well. Go in peace, and be healed of your affliction."

Mark 5:25–34

The Woman with the Issue of Blood

I am known as the woman with the
issue of blood in *The Book*.

For more than a decade, my health
and resources it took.

I tried every remedy and doctor around,

Then I heard Jesus of Nazareth was coming to town.

Word spread of the miracles He had done,

Like calming the storm and healing a son.

Never had I heard of a healer like this.

I must get to Him! I must take the risk!

It took all the strength I could muster up,

To get close enough for a minute touch.

Just as soon as His garment I reached,

Power raged through my body, and my bleeding
ceased!

He healed me completely and called me "daughter"
as well.

So, to everyone I meet, forever I will tell,

Jesus is my Master, my Healer, my Lord!

He is worthy of being praised and forever adored.

This passage is known as the story of the "woman with the issue of blood." Before we get to her encounter with Jesus, let's back up a bit and take a glimpse of *one* day in the life of Jesus. This one day reveals so much of His characteristics, His heart, and His power.

The narrative began with Jesus traveling by boat with His disciples. As they were crossing the Sea of Galilee, Jesus took a nap. While He was napping, a severe windstorm caused so much turbulence that the boat was taking on water. Fearing for their lives, the disciples woke Jesus, crying out, "Wake up! Help us! This boat is about to sink! We're all going to drown!"

Jesus awoke and calmly spoke to the wind and the sea. Immediately the wind ceased, and the sea was calm. The disciples were amazed, more like bewildered, and thinking, *Just who is this man and how was He able to do this?* What they had seen and heard was far more than their finite minds could appropriate. (See Luke 8:22–25.)

Before we become too judgmental, let's remember that they were living when biblical history was being made. At that time, there were no books or Bibles telling of Jesus' miracles. No teachers or pastors were yet declaring His works. Certainly, there were no radio or television programs to proclaim His deeds. Privileged as the disciples were to witness Jesus' miracles firsthand, it must have been overwhelming mentally, spiritually, and emotionally.

Now, back to the boat with the disciples and Jesus. The

next stop was in the country of the Gadarenes. As soon as they landed, Jesus was met by a wild man. Yes, an absolute wild man! He was possessed by many demons that gave him supernatural strength. He was so wild that he broke chains and shackles, lived in the cemetery, and ran around stark naked. Yes, he was truly *one hot mess*!

In this horrible condition, he fell on his knees in the presence of Jesus, recognizing Him as the "Son of the Most High God." Initially, that may seem like a strange response. However, when the forces of Satan come in contact with the Most High God, they realize they are overpowered. To make a long story short, Jesus showed compassion for the man and power over the demons. He commanded the demons to leave the man and enter a herd of pigs nearby. The pigs (controlled by the demons) then ran violently down an embankment and drowned in a lake. That is power! Selah. (See Luke 8:26–39.)

Next, Jesus moved to His intended audience, a crowd awaiting His presence and His message. Once again, He was interrupted. Before Jesus had the opportunity to greet those gathered, Jairus, a ruler of the synagogue, approached Him. Dropping to his knees, he begged Jesus for help. His only daughter (we don't know about any sons), twelve years old, was extremely sick. The father feared for her life. The heart of Jesus was touched with compassion for this father and his child. He started out to meet their need. On His way to the house of Jairus, a great crowd surrounded Him. It was from this large group of people that one unnamed woman made her way to Jesus.

Her Story

This dear woman was at the point of desperation. For more than a decade, twelve years to be exact, she had been plagued with a continuous bleeding problem. No relief, losing blood every day, every week, every month, for twelve years! I cannot imagine how weak she must have been at this point. I do understand having an issue of blood that controlled my life for one-fourth of the time, but not continuously. I will spare you the details. Suffice it to say, I went for years without a hemoglobin reading in two digits.

My situation could not be compared to hers. By this time in her life, this woman had to be fighting extreme discouragement. There she was, twelve years into this problem. Her finances were depleted. Her weakened condition was continually worsening. Add to this that the Jewish law also considered her ceremonially unclean, which added a layer of social isolation to her problem.

Digging Deeper

This woman was proactive—so much so that she had gone broke from paying the physicians available to her. None of them resolved her problem. Yet without any means of mass communication, the word of Jesus' miraculous healing power reached her ears.

When she heard that Jesus was coming to her area, faith rose up in her soul. If He could heal others, she felt confident He could also heal her. She viewed this as her *one*, perhaps her last, opportunity for hope. She *must* get to Jesus!

For years, I thought that her incident of healing was the only one that occurred by a simple touch of Jesus' garment. Then I came across these verses:

> *And when the men of that place recognized Him, they sent out into all the surrounding region, brought to Him all who were sick, and begged Him that they might only touch the hem of His garment. And as many as touched it were made perfectly well.*
>
> **Matthew 14:35–36**

> *Whenever He entered, into villages, cities, or the country, they laid the sick in the marketplaces, and begged Him that they might just touch the hem of His garment. And as many as touched Him were made well.*
>
> **Mark 6:56**

> *"And the whole multitude sought to touch Him, for power went out from Him and healed them all."*
>
> **Luke 6:19**

Assuming the stories in the Gospels are written in chronological order, a simple touch of Jesus' garment was quite commonplace for healing. That was exactly what this unnamed woman needed: to get close enough to Jesus to touch His clothing. Despite any effort, time, or energy involved, she *must* go. His touch just might be her means of healing!

With faith and determination, she planned her trip. We don't know how far she had to walk or how long it took her to get there in her weakened condition. Despite the difficulty, she had to keep going. I can imagine that every bit of her strength was depleted as she pushed through the crowd that day. By the time she drew near to Jesus, she may have been crawling and reaching out her hand with her last ounce of strength. Then it happened. She touched Jesus' robe or the tassels on the bottom of His prayer shawl. Immediately, at that very moment, she was healed. Elation cannot begin to describe her joy and relief! Strength once again flowed through her body. *She felt it!*

Jesus *felt it* too. He felt a measure of His healing power flow into someone who had reached out in faith. Unsure of exactly which person in the large group it was, Jesus said, "Who touched Me?'

Not knowing what that would mean for the person who had touched Him, I would dare to think there was a nervousness in the crowd. Perhaps many "not me" responses were given.

Then Jesus' disciple, the one known as impetuous Peter, spoke up. "Really, Jesus, in a group this size, there are many individuals who touched You, brushed by, or slightly bumped into You."

Jesus replied that it was not a casual, unintended swipe,

but someone had reached out in faith, and He *felt* power flow from Him.

Our unnamed woman knew she had to confess, but she was afraid. *What have I done?* she wondered. *Have I overstepped my social bounds by reaching out to this powerful rabbi? What will He say? What will He do?*

Nervously she bowed before Jesus, confessing her story to Him as well as to all those present. She told how she had arrived weak and needy. Then, with just a tiny touch of Jesus' garment, her healing was immediate and complete.

All her anxiety was dissolved as Jesus responded to her. He did not rebuke her as she had feared. His reply was *precious, positive,* and *peaceful.*

First, He addressed her as *daughter.* This is one of the most endearing terms we know. Like mother, father, son, sister, or brother, *daughter* signifies family, acceptance, love, and belonging. In calling her *daughter,* Jesus accepted her as one of the family, His child. How precious!

The word *daughter* certainly is very precious to me. I was blessed to be the daughter of wonderful parents who loved and provided for me. To the best of their ability, they surrounded my sister and me with love and all we needed. I am especially thankful for the wealth of spiritual opportunity they provided for us.

Jerry and I have one daughter and one son. Our daughter was our firstborn. I lovingly recall the joy she brought us the day she was born. Seeing Jerry happily holding her, parading proudly around the hospital room, is a cherished memory. There are hundreds of happy snapshots of her in my memory, as well as in our photo albums. I want to share one memory that expresses just how precious the word *daughter* is to me.

It was almost time for my seventieth birthday. Jerry had a drop-in planned for family and friends. All of our children and grandchildren lived at least seven hours away at that time; therefore, I did not expect to see any of them in person.

A day before the party, Jerry and I were heading home from shopping when our daughter called. She talked casually and asked when we expected to be home. We thought nothing of it. However, shortly after we arrived at the house, the doorbell rang. I looked outside and saw a car I did not recognize. As I peeked through the window, I could see part of a pink tee shirt. When I cracked the door open, my daughter, Amy, was standing right in front of me. I was totally speechless. I was so surprised that, initially, I forgot to ask her in. She has a picture of me standing there dazed! It was a priceless moment.

She had flown in from New Jersey and rented a car to be present for my big birthday. It was delightful. I don't remember exactly how long she stayed. I do know we had a wonderful visit the day before, the day of, and the day after my seventieth celebration. What a thoughtful surprise! I owe a debt of gratitude to her husband. He was left at home to manage the household and four kids while working at his job as well.

Amy has two daughters. They are our only granddaughters, and what a priceless relationship I have with each of them. (We also have five grandsons we love and adore. There are plenty of stories about them, but we are considering the term *daughter* for now.)

Daughters and granddaughters belong. They are family. They are a part of who we are. In this passage, Jesus attributes the title, *daughter*, to this one He healed on His way to the house of Jairus. In doing so, He expressed His precious love and acceptance.

Jesus' response to her was also positive. He said, "Be of good cheer. Look forward and cheer up because your future will be much better than your past. My healing touch has taken away your pain and weakness. You can now face the future with new strength and wellness. Yes, your future will be much more positive than your past."

Next, He probably said *shalom*, which has many meanings, but the most common translation is *peace*. By telling her to "go in peace," He was communicating, "I have given you My peace for your pain. Now that you have met Me and experienced My power, you know where to turn in time of need. Go in My peace, confident that I am only a prayer away."

Yes, He spoke to her in *precious, positive,* and *peaceful* tones. He also affirmed to her that it was faith that captured

His attention. Humanly, He was not aware of her presence that day until she extended her trembling hand in absolute faith. It was that reach of faith that connected her need with His omnipotent power. It is faith that pleases Him and brings Him to action. Throughout the Gospels, He declares healing takes place because of the faith the person exercised. As soon as this unnamed woman touched Jesus' clothing, her healing was immediate and complete.

We hear nothing more about this unnamed woman, only her one encounter with Jesus as recorded in two Gospels. I feel sure that with her burden lifted and body healed, she recounted the events of this one day to others for the rest of her life. What a day it was! Selah.

There were people with needs all around Jesus as He was on His way to heal the daughter of Jairus, yet He had time to reach out to *one* individual who came to Him in faith. He not only healed but also affirmed her.

For Jesus, the day was not yet over. He proceeded to the house of Jairus. There He raised the young girl from the dead! I stand amazed! Still, I'm not certain that was His last event of the day. Let us review the parts of His day we are aware of. He demonstrated His power to His disciples by calming a storm. From there, He freed the wild man from demon control. Our unnamed woman was then healed from her twelve-year bleeding disorder. All of that was to be followed by His raising a young girl from the dead! That was just one day of more than one thousand days in Jesus' three years of public ministry. No wonder the apostle John concluded his Gospel with this statement:

> *And there are also many other things that Jesus did, which if they were written one by one, I suppose that even the world itself could not contain the books that would be written. Amen!*

John 21:25

Selah! Take a moment to contemplate the power Jesus demonstrated in just this one day. It was more than our mortal minds can grasp or imagine. The last quotation recorded of Jesus was, "All authority has been given to Me in heaven and on earth" (Matthew 28:18). There is *no way* our finite minds can begin to assimilate the vastness of His power. It includes power to heal, power over Satan and his demons, power over death, power over nature, power to create, and so much more.

This power is inexhaustible! It has no end. So, if you are facing an impossibility today, reach out as this woman did. While He is not here physically to touch, you can reach out to Him with faith through prayer. Hebrews 13:8 states that He is the same today as He was in all of times past. Take a few moments to ponder the power He demonstrated in this one day. Selah! Surely there is absolutely *nothing* beyond the grasp of His power. He has the ability to transform your impossibility into a possibility.

God's ability can transform your impossibility into a possibility.

Call to Him in prayer. Then learn more of His ways from the Bible. Begin reading in Luke (I recommend Luke because it is my favorite Gospel) and Psalms. Proceed through the other Gospels (Matthew, Mark, and John) to see how Jesus *fleshed out* the characteristics of His heavenly Father. You will be amazed!

There are three lessons from this story we can apply to our daily lives.

First, we see that Jesus had time for individuals. As He moved among the people, He powerfully and compassionately reached out to those in great need. More than one unnamed person in this passage received His touch on this day. Despite the size of the crowd, He had time for each one. He *never* turned anyone away.

If you and I are to be His followers, we must have His help to be aware of the needs of our family members, neighbors, friends, and even strangers we come across from day to day. We need to give freely of our time and love to affirm others of their value.

Prayer

Lord Jesus, give me a heart of compassion like Yours. When I have the wherewithal or ability, let me *not* pass by anyone I can encourage or give a helping hand. Show me the individual. Show me the need. Give me courage to obey Your leading. Amen.

Second, we are challenged by the proactive measures taken by our unnamed woman. The Scripture states that before reaching out to Jesus, she had emptied her resources seeking help from those in the medical community. On this day of her healing, she expended all her strength to get to Jesus. It is entirely possible that she began her attempt to reach Jesus as soon as she was aware of His power to heal and His plan to come to a location near her.

However, I wonder how often we try everything else to fix our problem *before* taking it to the Lord Jesus. It is human nature to attempt to solve our own situations. But oh, how much anxiety we could prevent by committing our needs to Him in prayer first rather than as "the last resort." He is always awake and on duty. We just need to A-S-K, ask, seek, and knock.

Prayer

Lord, help me so grow in the knowledge of Your power that I will call out to You first and foremost. Help me to avoid confusion and wasted time while seeking solutions on my own or from other sources. You have all power and all knowledge. It is reasonable for me, Your child, to seek Your wisdom in every situation *first*. Thank You for Your patience extended to me as I am learning this truth. Amen.

Third, we observed that Jesus spoke to our unnamed woman in *precious*, *positive*, and *peaceful* tones. I don't know about you, but I have a long way to go in following this example. Psalm 141:3 is a guide for me: "Set a guard, O Lord, over my mouth. Keep watch over the door of my lips."

Prayer

Lord, I need You to instruct me in speaking words that value my hearers. Help me extend a place of comfort and acceptance to everyone who crosses my path in life. Teach me to leave every person with the positive hope of Your guidance, assured that life can be lived in *precious*, *positive*, and *peaceful* days as we trust in You. Amen.

Personal Response

Place the following in 1, 2, 3 order (1 being what needs the most work, then 2, and 3 in descending order, those needing less improvement).

_____ Speaking words of affirmation and acceptance.

_____ Seeking God's help first, not as a last resort.

_____ Being alert to the needs of others, not passing them by.

Write your own prayer and/or action plan for responding more and more like Jesus in these three areas.

_____

_____

_____

_____

_____

While writing about Jesus' compassion for the individual, I remembered this poem I wrote years ago. I hope it will become the prayer of your heart.

A Heart of Compassion

Lord Jesus, the more at Your life I look,

I see a heart of compassion and no need You ever forsook.

You had time for the lonely, sick, and forlorn,

Giving help and compassion to everyone born.

You reached out to heal those others would not come near.

To those outcasted You called "daughter" or said, "Come here!"

Lord Jesus, as I read and study Your ways,

I see love and compassion filling Your days.

To all who were hurting, alone, or in sin,

You reached out to help, heal, and defend.

You were never too busy to show compassion and care.

Oh, what it must have been like to see You there!

Lord Jesus, You know today we run, and we go,

Hurriedly passing others, too busy to show

The love and concern You'd have us to.

But Lord, I want a heart of. compassion like You!

I want to be the one who shows love and care

When others may not notice a person is there.

Give me Your compassion to sense the need.

Help me to be willing to give a hand, a prayer, a deed.

I don't want to pass those hurting on life's path.

I want Your heart of compassion to give help that lasts!

CHAPTER SEVEN

THE UNNAMED

Persistent Widow

.

Then He spoke a parable to them, that men always ought to pray and not lose heart, saying: "There was in a certain city a judge who did not fear God nor regard man. Now there was a widow in that city; and she came to him, saying 'Get justice for me from my adversary.' And he would not for a while; but afterward he said within himself, 'Though I do not fear God nor regard man, yet because this widow troubles me I will avenge her, lest by her continual coming she weary me.'" Then the Lord said, "Hear what the unjust judge said. And shall God not avenge His own elect who cry out day and night to Him, though He bears long with them? I tell you that He will avenge them speedily. Nevertheless, when the Son of Man comes, will He really find faith on the earth?"

Luke 18:1–8

The Persistent Widow

A parable is a story Jesus told to teach a lesson true.

It helps us understand His way and tells us what to do.

In Luke 18, He says we should always pray and never lose heart.

Just keep on seeking Him, and God will do His part.

He has all the answers. He has all power,

And *that* we know for sure.

Some answers come right away,

For others, we must endure.

He is never late, though we may wait,

He never sleeps or slumbers.

He knows our hearts, He knows our needs,

And sends blessings without number.

The writer of Luke clearly states that this is a parable rather than an actual occurrence. A parable is an earthly story with a heavenly meaning. It is a simple story Jesus used to teach a moral or spiritual lesson. This parable, *The Persistent Widow*, teaches believers that to avoid discouragement, we should pray persistently and consistently.

Her Story

This story has two main characters: An evil judge who had neither honor for God nor respect for his fellow man, and a widow who came before the judge with a request for help. The widow had been involved in a conflict that required a mediator. We assume that she had attempted every other method of resolution she knew, but nothing worked. In desperation, she made her appeal to the judge for help. Perhaps she knew only of his position but not his character.

When she first came to the judge, he was dismissive. He had no time for the likes of her. This was not a satisfactory response for the woman. She needed help beyond her personal abilities, so she returned to plead her case with him, time and time again. Her persistence was an annoyance to the judge. Strictly to make her go away, he finally responded to her request.

Digging Deeper

Jesus tells us to hear, consider, or listen to what the unjust judge said, "Though I do not fear God nor regard man, yet because this widow troubles me I will avenge her, lest by her continual coming she weary me." Notice that the words *I* and *me* are mentioned four times in that brief quotation. The judge showed absolutely no concern for the widow. It was out of his selfish motivation that he gave in to her request. Wow! The lesson I learned from this example is that when God's people rely on Him in continual prayer, He can turn around the heart of the vilest and most wicked person to show favor to a believer. Yes, God melted the cold, hard heart of an official to make a way for His child. Selah! What an encouragement and comfort that is.

God, the Father, bears absolutely no resemblance to the unjust judge in this passage. He asks, invites, and commands His children to call out to Him. Contrary to the example of this self-serving judge, our reliance on our Father gives Him delight. He is never annoyed by our cries. He never sleeps and is ever listening to our prayers. Truly, He is awesome!

Awesome became a buzzword several years back. Anything could be considered awesome: tennis shoes, a new hairdo, a steak. While those may be nice, *awesome* really is when you or I view God as all-powerful in His person, His work, or His creation. Awesome is my dumbfounded, wordless response to His holiness and power. All His attributes are beyond our human comprehension. Our silent pause to contemplate His majesty gives us a glimpse of *awe*!

I was made aware of this truth several years ago while

driving to school in the mornings. Each day I had to navigate a curve that was almost a ninety-degree angle. Within that curve, there was a beautiful sunrise almost every day. Being alone, I would tell the Lord aloud how impressed I was with His creation. I would comment on the colors and how different one day's sunrise was from another. These were glorious moments, just God and me. One day He spoke this truth to me: "All My attributes are limitless." Selah! That was a fantastic revelation! I had time "to Selah" that all the way to school. Truly, I was awestruck. As I contemplated that truth He communicated, I began to realize that He never runs out of anything: not colors or hues, not ideas, not compassion, not varied and beautiful sunrises. *All* His attributes are *never-ending*! He never runs short on mercy, forgiveness, love, peace, creativity, ideas, comfort, or any other of His infinite characteristics!

All His attributes are never-ending!

This lesson was made even clearer to me a few years back when Jerry and I had the opportunity to spend a beautiful summer day at the beach with our son and grandson. Our grandson was about four years old at the time. He and his dad enjoyed a delightful time splashing in the waves. Then they built a sand structure surrounded by a moat. What a delight it was to watch my grandson go back and forth from the beach to the water's edge, hauling pails of water for the moat. Observing this, I realized that little Ryan got all the water he could manage. At the same time, he thoroughly enjoyed the process of running back and forth from beach to ocean. Joyfully, he had more than enough. Yet, when I looked across the majestic ocean, it was not diminished at all. The waters of the seas still covered approximately two-thirds of the earth. What a parallel to the attributes of God. Every one of them is inexhaustible. Selah! Throughout the ages, no matter how much of any one of His attributes mankind has withdrawn, the supply is *never*-ending. His mercies are without limit. This is the truly awesome God to whom we pray. Give Him praise. He is worthy! Selah!

He is the ultimate Father who loves His children without limit. He delights in answering our prayers and providing for us all. He says, "Call to Me, and I will answer you, and show you great and mighty things, which you do not know" (Jeremiah 33:3). Yes, call to Me in prayer with what you think is needed. I promise to answer. Since My knowledge and resources far exceed yours, I may just blow your mind and answer in a way that you could not even imagine. I *am* the great I *am*. I *am* omniscient. I *am* omnipotent. So, ask!

Remember Matthew 7:7–8,

> *Ask, and it will be given to you; seek, and you will find; knock, and it will be opened to you.*

For everyone who asks receives, and he who seeks finds, and to him who knocks it will be opened.

These are promises for you and me. Our Holy God cannot go back on His promises. So, whatever you are experiencing right now, ask, seek, knock. Then find a scripture that fits the situation; post it on your mirror or refrigerator (whichever one you frequent most). Read it repeatedly. Commit it to memory. Carry it on a 3x5 card. Pray it. His words are true and unfailing.

We live in a microwave era. We expect our problems to be solved and our needs to be met instantly. Sometimes that is the case. Whew! What a relief! Other times that is not the case. At this writing, Jerry and I are anticipating a situation to be changed for which we were given a promise twelve years ago. It is coming soon. I believe it! The waiting is *not* easy. Verse 7 in our original passage (Luke 18) indicates that there will be times when we "cry out day and night to Him." There is time involved. God hears us and bears long with us. That is, He walks through the unknown with us. As our loving, heavenly Father, He teaches and comforts us as we wait for the promise to be fulfilled. I like verse 8a: "I tell you that He will avenge them speedily." There will come an end to the problem that seems never-ending to us. It may endure for a long period of time, then end suddenly. Remember how Joseph endured injustices for years, then suddenly he was called to stand before the king. *That day* he was made second-in-command in Egypt. Selah. (Genesis 41)

This gives me hope that there will be a speedy resolution to our situation. So, we keep praying and don't lose heart or become discouraged. Truly, He knows our needs before we ask, yet He desires our love and our communication with Him as we wait. We walk through our days, breathing dependence on Him hour by hour.

There are times to be on our knees in prayer. There are times to be in solitude while praying but *praying without ceasing* looks more like walking through life, literally breathing our dependence, belief, and honor moment by moment. It is a life of acknowledging Him, thanking Him, and loving Him. I can think of at least three women who have exemplified this moment-by-moment reliance on the Lord. I have been inspired by being around these women, hearing them pray, and hearing their stories.

The mother of one of my best, lifelong friends has been widowed for years. Her life of solitude is lived talking to the Lord, seeking His guidance as well as giving Him honor. It is constant communication. She talks to Him about everything, not just major decisions but mundane things such as, "Should I go now?" "Should I buy this?" "Is this a good time to mow the lawn?" At ninety-four years old, she still uses a riding lawnmower. That is a good reason to be advised from above. She is forever muttering her thanks. Her total dependence is a beautiful thing to witness. She sets quite an example to follow.

Certainly, there are times when silent prayers are necessary. There are times when we find ourselves just muttering (barely audible, like when my husband is driving!) prayers to our Lord. However, I feel there is something powerful about praying aloud. The Scriptures are replete with commands to call, cry out, shout, praise, sing, ascribe, bless, extol, and declare when communicating with the Lord. He is not deaf. He even knows our thoughts. Crying out to the Lord is cathartic for us and a blessing to Him.

We need to hear our own declarations and scriptures we are claiming. Speaking out loud helps us stay focused and to hear the words of Scripture repeated. As we lay our souls open before Him, we sense His presence. Then it is good to pause and be silent, awaiting any message or direction from Him. The more we pray, the more God is magnified in our thinking. We experience Him working in our lives through situations both big and small. He shows us that nothing is too complex for Him to handle. Neither is anything too small for His concern.

> *The more we pray, the more God is magnified in our thinking.*

He leads us to the house that is perfect for our family. He heals our wounds from a car accident. He guides our children and us to the school of His choice. Nothing is too difficult for Him. Yet, He tenderly puts a prayerful individual in our path just when we need a prayer and a hug. He helps us find the keys or the document that we absentmindedly misplaced. He allows us to find the last one of a super discounted item. Nothing is too small for His concern. He never sleeps. Therefore, He is on duty always to care for His children.

Prayer is much more than pleading with God to resolve our problems. It is worship. When Jesus set forth the pattern for prayer known as *The Lord's Prayer*, worship took priority. The first phrases give honor to God the Father, acknowledge His holiness and His rule, as well as the prayer's total dependence on Him for all things. In today's vernacular, we might say, "Lord God, Holy Father in heaven, I come to You desiring to cooperate with You that Your way may be done in my life, that is, in my world and surroundings, as it is in Yours. You are the only one on whom I can depend in every situation..." then continue with petitions.

Thanksgiving is another vital component of prayer. Taking time to enumerate God's blessing is life-transforming. Four or five years ago, Jerry introduced "10,000 reasons (Bless the Lord)" by Matt Redman to the congregation where we were serving. I knew the song. Loved it! Yet that day, I was challenged in my heart. I wondered just how long it would take to list 10,000 of the Lord's blessings to me. I took a spiral notebook, divided the pages into three columns, and began. I did not become a slave to this task. At least two, maybe three times a week, I would sit and reflect upon His goodness to me. Once I started, there was no stopping. James 1:17 states that "every good gift and every perfect gift is from above." Therefore, *every* relationship, *every*thing of beauty, *every* food, *every* ability, and so much more is a reason for thanksgiving. Oh, by the way, it took me close to two and a half years to get to 10,000. Presently I am at 18,000. Now I see His hand everywhere I go. My gratitude keeps growing.

I challenge you to take a few minutes to list His gifts to you. If you need some help, look outside. What do you see that God alone created? Look inside. What comforts and conveniences are in your home that millions around the world would be thrilled to have? Look at your body. Every working part or system is a blessing. List them. How about your family? Your relationships? Your church family? Insights into the Word of God? If you use just these few suggestions for a starting point, it won't take long to list 100–200 reasons for thanksgiving. Soon you will be on your way to 1,000! Giving thanks will become a way of life.

In the King James Version of the Bible (KJV), Luke 18:1b states, "Men ought always to pray, and not to faint." Have you ever fainted? I have on several occasions. It is not a pleasant experience. One moment you're fully functional, alert, and aware. Then, unknowingly, you fall or lose consciousness. When you awake in another place, you don't know how you got there or how much time has elapsed.

Many years ago, when Jerry was finishing his college hours, we lived in a tiny basement apartment near the university. One day, I went upstairs to pay the rent. I remember standing at the kitchen counter talking with our landlady. My next recollection was being on a sofa in another room. I still have no idea how that short, small-framed lady got me to that place. My mind was foggy and confused. What happened? How did I get here? What time was it? All these were unanswered questions. The point is that fainting puts you out of touch with reality for a time. This is not the condition in which believers should live. Jesus is teaching in this passage that to prevent living in a confused stupor, we should be in a constant attitude of prayer and dependence. There is so much that vies for our attention: TV, iPad, multi-media devices, newspapers, magazines, and even conversations tend to pull our minds into thinking patterns contrary to Jesus' ways.

In essence, Jesus is saying, "Pray always and don't lose heart, become discouraged, hopeless, or faint." Prayer puts our focus on our Father and His goodness. We get a glimpse of His might, His love, and His benevolence throughout the universe and to us as individuals. With Him exalted in our hearts and minds, we can face life's uncertainties in His presence. Selah! Even on difficult days, we can have hope that defeats discouragement. We are alert, alive, walking with our hand in His, totally aware that with Him, *nothing* is impossible. Truly that is abundant living! What a terrific lesson we can ponder from this brief passage. Selah.

Jesus concludes this passage with what seems to me to be a rather unusual question: "Nevertheless, when the Son of

Man comes, will He really find faith on the earth?" As the omniscient Son of God, He lives beyond the boundaries of time as we know it. Perhaps He had an instant snapshot into the future and questioned if there would be those who truly rely on Him in all of life's situations or, comparatively speaking, just how many believing persons will there be in comparison to the nonbelievers when He returns? Remember, I don't claim to be a Bible scholar, so I am not sure if this is quantitative or qualitative.

When I was growing up, most people in my community either believed the Word of God and went to church, or they had respect for those who did. Unbelievers knew to whom to turn for answers in their time of trouble. They honored the people of God, the Word of God, and the house of God. Vandalism and robbery of churches were totally unheard of. Believers felt freedom of expression and were not threatened or intimidated by unbelievers. My, how these values have changed over time.

I want you to meet my dad. While imperfect as any of us, he lived out what he believed. He was a World War II veteran who witnessed and experienced the hell of war! He saw hundreds of Americans hanging from trees in Germany. He was forced to sit on a corpse to eat his rations while smelling the decay around him. He experienced the fear and danger of being in a foxhole. He knew well the horror of overhead shelling and being wedged under a Jeep for cover. The cold was so intense as he marched toward the Battle of the Bulge that he and other soldiers forced livestock out of barns so they could thaw out under the warm straw. It was in this extreme cold that my dad's feet froze black. This was far worse than frostbite! It was so bad that the medics wanted to amputate. He declined the surgery because he was assured of the prayers of his parents back home. God answered those prayers, and he walked on those feet for more than sixty years.

My dad knew what it was like to be the only one of approximately 175 men in his company who did not engage in sexual activity while abroad. In the chest pocket of his uniform, he carried a New Testament given to him by his mother, as well as a picture of my mother and my sister, who was a beautiful eighteen-month-old when he left. These served as reminders of his beliefs and loyalties, as well as his determination to live and return home to those he loved.

I am not sure at what point during the horrors of war my dad made a vow to the Lord. He later told us that he said something like, *Lord, if You will get me out of here and home safely, I will serve You the remaining days of my life*. Understandably, many soldiers uttered such words when faced with death. For my dad, this was not an empty, meaningless promise. He meant it! I was privileged to see what it looked like for him to live out this vow.

Thankfully, he did return home safely (or I would not be here). He lived as a loving and faithful husband, father, son, brother, and eventually granddaddy of five. Always learning and growing in his faith walk, he delighted in giving his time, abilities, and resources to the cause of

Christ in his church. He had a small produce business. Without a doubt, his customers were aware of his faith in Christ. He spoke of his Lord often, gave out hundreds of gospel tracts, and sang or hummed hymns as he worked. In his later years, he became a patient (frequent flyer) at the VA Hospital in Atlanta, fighting multiple illnesses, including cancer. As long as he had the strength to do so, he went from room to room and bed to bed with a witness for Jesus. He would give a word of encouragement, a prayer, or a gospel tract to all who would receive it.

Toward the end of his life, my dad was confined to bed because his leg had broken due to the spread of cancer. By that time, there was no way to reset it. His bones were too compromised. One day when several of his family members visited, we asked him what he wanted us to do: sing, pray, read from the Bible? He chose prayer with him leading. I will never forget how he gave thanks and then prayed for his neighbor who had not come to Jesus. He never mentioned himself or his pain. It was a prayer from a grateful heart and concern for others.

Oh yes, I'd say my dad kept his vow. He was an ordinary man from "the greatest generation." He kept his promise. It guided the remainder of his life. He truly loved telling the story of Jesus. That is the reason why I burst into tears when I hear the song "I Love to Tell the Story." For most people, it is not a particularly emotional song, but it always will be for me. These words were so true of my dad.

I love to tell the story
Of unseen things above,
Of Jesus and His glory,
Of Jesus and His love.
I love to tell the story
Because I know it's true.
It satisfies my longings
As nothing else can do.
I love to tell the story,
'Tis pleasant to repeat.
What seems each time I tell it,
More wonderfully sweet.
I love to tell the story;
For some have never heard
The message of salvation
From God's own holy Word.
I love to tell the story,
'Twill be my thee in glory.
To tell the old, old story
Of Jesus and His love.
(Public domain)

I recently heard that the world's population is approaching eight billion. While there are millions here in America and around the world who love and serve our Lord, we might seem like a remnant compared to all who are not believers. To answer His question, Jesus asked, "Will He find faith on the earth when He returns?" Let's answer *yes*! So long as there are others around like my daddy, the answer is *yes*. Let's you and I pledge to be two who are walking in dependence on Him, willing to share His words and ways. We just might be here when He comes back. How exciting that would be!

Meanwhile, our faith, prayers, and influence could be just the *mortar* that *matters* that provides a connection to the Lord for one, twenty, fifty, or many hundreds of individuals as we also consistently live out our vows to Him.

Personal Response

As you contemplate the lessons from this chapter, rate yourself on a scale of 1 to 5 in the following areas:

1. I talk to Him about *every* situation in life, both big and small.

    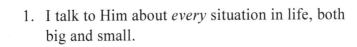

    1   2   3   4   5

2. I thank Him daily for His abundant blessings to me.

    1   2   3   4   5

3. My prayer life is growing as I see answers to prayers. I am also learning to wait.

    1   2   3   4   5

Prayer

Father God, I am amazed by Your unlimited power, Your vast goodness, and Your knowledge of me, one ordinary person. I am thankful that You have showered me with blessings. (Name some.) Thank You, for You are *always* available! Forgive me for ignoring Your presence, Your creation, and Your power in times past. Teach me to "pray always" and not to walk in self-pity or in discouragement. Teach me Your ways that I may shine forth Your light and Your love to those around me. I desire for others to see Your likeness in me as I go about my everyday responsibilities. Now I sit here quietly to give You my love and praise.

Amen.

Here is a poem the Lord gave me as I was contemplating the subject of prayer. I hope it is encouraging to you.

Talk to Me, My Child

Talk to Me. Talk to Me always, My child.

I hear you night and day. I hear you all the while.

I love to hear your voice. I love to hear your praise.

And I never object when your hands are raised.

You are Mine. You are My very own.

You are always welcome to come before My throne.

I am never too busy or too far away.

Morning, noon, or night, I love to hear you pray.

Your problems are never too big, nor are they too small.

My ears are always open to hear your every call.

So don't waste your time with worry and fret,

Not one child of Mine has been forsaken yet.

Talk to Me. Talk to Me always, My child.

I hear you night and day. I hear you all the while.

CHAPTER EIGHT

THE UNNAMED

Woman with the Alabaster Box

173

And when Jesus was in Bethany at the house of Simon the leper, a woman came to Him having an alabaster flask of very costly fragrant oil, and she poured it on His head as He sat at the table. But when His disciples saw it, they were indignant, saying, "Why this waste? For this fragrant oil might have been sold for much and given to the poor." But when Jesus was aware of it, He said to them, "Why do you trouble the woman? For she has done a good work for Me. For you have the poor with you always, but Me you do not have always. For in pouring this fragrant oil on My body, she did it for My burial. Assuredly, I say to you, wherever this gospel is preached in the whole world, what this woman has done will also be told as a memorial to her."

Matthew 26:6–13

The Woman with the Alabaster Box

Jesus went to Bethany to meet with friends,

To share a meal before the day's end.

In came a woman with a flask in her hand,

Containing expensive perfume

Others did not understand.

Why did she come?

Why was she here?

As she approached Jesus, her motive was clear.

The container of perfume she broke open and poured

All of it over the head of her Lord!

Wasteful! Wasteful! Others cried out.

This could have been sold, and without a doubt,

Many of the poor could have been helped out

Jesus said, "Leave her alone. Let her be!"

"Her generous gift brings honor to Me!

She came to express love while she could,

To lavishly give to Me as few people would.

From this time on, wherever My story is told.

This woman shall be remembered for what she gave,

Not what she sold."

Matthew, Mark, Luke, and John: all four Gospels give an account of a woman coming to Jesus with a lavish gift of perfume. Matthew and Mark have extremely similar narratives. Luke and John give additional details and applications. Some believe this indicates two different events, while others believe it is simply varied accounts of the same incident. For our consideration, we will look at the narrative from Matthew and Mark to see what insights we can glean from those passages.

Just prior to this story, Jesus had been teaching, healing, and doing many miracles among the people. He told His followers of prophecies that would be fulfilled. He even told them of His impending death and resurrection. He was loving, caring, and doing the impossible, yet there were adversaries plotting to destroy Him. Yes, despite all His compassion and positive deeds, they were planning to *kill* Him. Hard to believe! Yet, because it was the time of the highly celebrated Feast of the Passover, the schemers delayed their evil plan.

Her Story

It was at that time Jesus went to Bethany. There He was having dinner at the home of Simon the leper, father of Mary, Martha, and Lazarus. As Jesus and His friends were relaxing at the table, an unidentified woman arrived. She was carrying a flask (or box) of extremely expensive perfume. As she approached Jesus, she broke open the container and emptied the entire contents over His head.

She came to express her love, honor, and appreciation to Him alone. It was her moment to give her best—her most valued possession—to Him. There is no indication that she sought the attention of others in the room. However, the disciples reacted immediately.

"What a waste!" was their quick response to her selfless deed. "This perfume is expensive! Don't you know it could have been sold for a tremendous price? The proceeds from its sale could have been used to help many in need." Basically, they were communicating, "Why would you *waste* all this on *one* individual when the money derived from its sale could have been extended to *many*."

Were these men already involved in benevolence to the poor, or were they simply being judgmental? Rather than enjoying the fragrance that filled the room or appreciating the honor the woman gave Jesus, they jumped to their own biased conclusions.

Jesus did not share their views. As the Son of God, He knew the *present*. He saw the heart of the woman. Her worship and her love were exactly what He needed at that moment in time.

He also knew the *future*. He knew that very soon He would be facing betrayal, abuse, and agony *alone*! Alone as no other human has ever experienced. Selah. While He was enduring the horrendous pain of the penalty for the sin of mankind, even God the Father turned away from Jesus. We can only hope that during this darkest hour of human history, a faint whiff of the perfume possibly offered Him a glimmer of comfort, even a momentary reminder of the love that had been expressed to Him only days before.

Although Jesus had told His followers He would die and rise from the dead, they had absolutely *no* way of understanding that. This woman had no way of envisioning her gift of perfume would possibly bring a measure of comfort to her dying Savior as wafts of fragrance emitted from His hair and beard as He suffered through His trial and crucifixion. She simply was doing what she could and giving her very best.

At this point, once again, Jesus reminded those present that He would not always be with them. Opportunity to minister to Him physically was extremely temporary. However, there would never be a time when poverty would be irradiated. For all of time, there would be many in need of help.

How true that is. No matter the country or the century we live in, there will always be poverty. The causes are many. In some areas, there isn't adequate fertile land or rain to produce the food needed for all the inhabitants. There are many places where there is not sufficient job opportunity. Wars and corruption in government cause poverty. Catastrophes, such as floods, hurricanes, fires, earthquakes, tornadoes, and other disasters, result in poverty as well. Any one of these can wipe out all resources for thousands of people. When people lose all their possessions, it is far beyond difficult to recover. It takes years to resume any measure of normality. Since there is no way to prevent disasters, poverty will always exist. Jesus said so.

The needs of others as they pass through trials give us believers the opportunity to flesh out our faith. We know that greed and self-centeredness should never characterize our life. Instead, we should be givers. When we are aware of others barely eking out an existence, we should gladly extend a hand of mercy.

Giving is much like a saturated sponge. It is impossible to hand it off to someone else and not get wet yourself. Luke 6:38 affirms this concept.

> *Give, and it will be given to you: good measure, pressed down, shaken together, and running over will be put into your bosom. For with the same measure that you use, it will be measured back to you.*

Basically, that verse says when you give, you will have a return. What you give, you will be blessed with in return. The same measure of generosity you give will be used to bless you in return. According to this one verse from Scripture, giving is a win-win situation. Not only does our giving meet the needs of others, but it also brings joy and blessing to the giver as well.

Jesus accepted the woman's gift. She gave the most valuable item she possessed. She gave it all, not reserving even a portion for herself. This so touched the heart of Jesus that He wanted her generosity to be remembered for all time. He told those there that day something like this, "Not only will I never forget this extravagant gift, but I want this deed of love to be memorialized. Wherever and whenever My story is told, I want people to know what this woman did for Me at a pivotal point in My life. What she did was a comforting deed for Me, for My body, and for My burial." (See Matthew 26:12.)

As we have witnessed the destruction of monuments and memorials recently, I find it notable that Jesus believed in memorials. The honor and gratitude this woman demonstrated touched Him so deeply that He wanted everyone throughout the ages to know of her expression of love. We may not know her name, but her action lives on and on.

Good deeds are often referred to as "alms" in the Bible. We are instructed not to call attention to self while doing good. Quietly, even anonymously, "alms" should be a constant outflow of a believer's life. In thinking about this, I have concluded that the memory of "alms" lives on far after the deed. While the giver may forget the deed, the giving lives in the memory of the recipient. Let me give you some examples of why I come to this conclusion.

One of my very favorite meals is old-fashioned, Southern-style biscuits and gravy. Jerry and I pass a Bojangles on our way to and from church. (In case you are not familiar, Bojangles is a fast-food restaurant that specializes in fried chicken and amazing biscuits.) Biscuits crunchy and golden on the outside and warm and fluffy on the inside!

I *love* those biscuits!

One Sunday morning, Jerry asked if I would object to stopping by Bojangles on our way home from church to pick up some gravy biscuits. Oh boy! That surely sounded great to me! With that plan in motion, we stopped to treat ourselves after church. There was a long line of cars with other folks awaiting some of this good Southern fare. The backup was due to the fact that the early church service had just ended, plus it was drive-through only because of COVID-19. Dutifully, we got in line and waited ten to thirteen minutes. Then a man in a pickup truck came around the opposite side of the building seeking a place in the line. Since we had waited so long already, I mumbled some comment about passing him by. I was kindly rebuked by my husband, who allowed the guy to go ahead of us.

Our wait continued another ten minutes or more. Finally, when we approached the window, the clerk confirmed our order and proceeded to tell us we owed nothing. The man in the pickup truck had paid our tab! Delighted but somewhat chagrined, we headed home to enjoy our delicious meal. We will never be able to thank that stranger, but do you think for a moment we will ever forget his good deed? No way, because every time we pass by Bojangles, we will remember this man. I believe the memory of "alms" lasts forever, or at least for a long time.

In contemplating this concept, I remembered *long* ago. More than forty years ago, I had two miscarriages. At the time of the first one, Jerry took me to the emergency entrance of the local hospital. Shortly thereafter, he went to park the car. At the receiving desk, a soft-spoken older gentleman was on duty. He perceived that I was hemorrhaging and saw that I got to triage quickly. His eyes were kind. His voice was comforting. His knowledge was reassuring. He did not panic. He kindly and competently got me the care I needed. Will I ever forget that man? I think not because it has been closer to fifty than forty years now, and I still remember his care for me. Memory of deeds of kindness can last forever.

My birthday is at the end of August, and Jerry's is at the end of September. Ever since her retirement, his sweet sister plans to visit us during that time frame. We have a great time visiting, going down memory lane, laughing, and playing games together. The highlight of the visit is a dinner out: her treat.

This year she came, and we made a plan for our "outing." The options were fewer because of COVID-19. We were more excited than usual due to the rarity of restaurant experiences of late. The three of us entered our chosen restaurant in a joyful, or maybe even a little rowdy, manner.

We asked the hostess for a waitress who had previously served us with warmth and kindness. Yes! She was on duty. We asked her to seat us as far away from others as possible. (Again, COVID-19.) We had a fun time together and enjoyed a wonderful meal. When the waitress returned with our bill, it was marked, "Happy Birthday! Paid in full!"

Surprised, delighted, elated! Yes, we experienced all those emotions. We looked around. We had *no* idea who paid that tab. We had *no* way to thank them, but do you think we will ever forget that deed of kindness? No way! I believe that the memory of "alms" has a way of lasting forever!

Referencing this unnamed woman's deed in Mark 8, Jesus said, "She has done what she could." Every time I read that verse, that statement speaks to my heart. "She has done what she could." Oh, I desire He could say that of me! She couldn't do everything, but what she could, she poured her life into with gusto.

During my childhood years and even throughout high school, I was extremely shy. I was comfortable withdrawing from a crowd, making myself as invisible as possible. Because of this lack of confidence, it was easy for me to say and believe, "I can't," when asked to do anything. Thankfully, with the help of my husband, I have come out of my shell (maybe too much!). I have learned that the more I'm willing to stretch my abilities, the more they expand.

I am very thankful our parents provided piano lessons for my sister and me. I also took some lessons during my college days. I'd say I'm an "okay" player and strictly by note. But I really love to hear Dino Kartsonakis, Kim Collingsworth, Gordon Mote, and Anthony Burger play. How I wish I had their ability and skill. According to Matthew 25:14–29, I'd say they were given the "five talents." In comparison, I was given only "one talent." Since I'm only a so-so player, is it okay for me not to play at all? No! There are small venues such as retirement homes, small groups, and here at home with my grandchildren, where I can use my limited ability to spread gladness to others. God expects me to do what I can do, not what I wish I could do.

I carried the following quotation in my wallet for years. Over time, I lost it, only to come across it recently. (Found in a letter from Carol, my late, dear friend from my college days.)

> *I am only one;*
> *...I cannot do everything;*
> *But still I can do something;*
> *And because I cannot do everything,*
> *I will not refuse to do something that I can do.*
> *[Selah!]*
>
> **Edward Everett Hale**

God expects me to do what I can do, not what I wish I could do.

How easy it is to make excuses. Legitimately, we realize there are others who can do almost anything better than we can. With that in mind, we often opt out by saying,

185

"I can't" or "If only I could do that as well as Mrs. So-N-So, then maybe I would try." The truth is no one of us is empty-handed. God has given each of us a measure of something we *can* use to bless another person or persons. No excuses: you are not too old, too young, too limited, too anything. You *are* who God made you with the abilities He chose to include in your person.

With that thought in mind, let me share with you a poem I wrote several years ago. I was sitting on the couch in our den when, out of nowhere, a yodel came to mind. I heard "little ole lady who," and immediately, the Lord gave me the following thoughts.

Little Old Lady, Who

Are you thinking,
I have less future and a lot more past
In the world's view?
I'm old and retired, what can I do?
What can I offer God's kingdom today?
I'm wrinkled, saggy, and my hair's turned gray!
Wrong thinking! Wrong thinking!
Change your mind.
Look all around you, and you will find,
Those in abundance who are young yet confused.
Never, never say you can't be used...
To bring love and directions to those near your door
Who are struggling and searching,
But they don't know what for.
Reflect, reflect on what God has brought you through.
Praise Him and ask Him still to use you.
Look! Look! What's in your hand?
Is it a paintbrush, a trowel, or a muffin pan?
Offer it up as a sacrifice to the Lord.
He will use it to bless others and to bring them on board.
Little Old Lady, Little Old Lady, who!
Never think there's nothing left for you.
Give, give every day of your life.
Give of your prayers, experiences, your strife.
Place them all in the Master's hand.
Let Him use them, and His glory expand.
Little Old Lady, Little Old Lady, who!
Until your last breath,
There will always be a place in God's
Harvest field for you!

Our unnamed woman gave lavishly! Without question, the alabaster box or flask of fragrant oil was the item of highest monetary value she owned. It may have been the one thing she had saved or treasured for years. We have no way of knowing. Since we are not positive about who this lady was, we are not certain of the circumstances that prompted her lavish gift to Jesus. We perceive that some internal motivation gave her the impetus to pour out her treasure in reckless abandon. She did not drip or sprinkle. She *poured* her treasure out to Jesus. Whether a flask or an alabaster box, she cracked it open and literally dumped the entire content on Jesus. None was left for her future enjoyment. Her gift was lavish, over the top!

We know we are to be consistent givers as a part of our obedience to Christ. However, there may be times when, like this woman, we are impressed to give a large amount of money or a highly valued commodity. While she gave perfume, we might be asked to give our used car to someone rather than using it for a trade-in or down payment. We might be prompted to give an extra $50, $100, $500, or even more to a worthy cause or struggling individual.

It could be surgery or a water well we are asked to finance. The opportunities are endless. No matter what we are called upon to give, it could be just the item or just the amount that turns someone's life around. What a privilege to cooperate with the God of the universe to make life changes happen. Selah! Lavish can be large and costly. Lavish can also be small and without monetary value.

When our daughter was in early elementary school, she attended a private, Christian school. One morning, while in her chapel service, a missionary speaker told of the meager existence the children in his country of service had to endure. The story gripped my daughter's little heart. She came home and announced that she was giving "Kathy" to the missionary to take back to some impoverished child. I was shocked. We were barely getting by at that time; therefore, she did not have an abundance of toys. But her mind was set. She cleaned and dressed her doll, "Kathy." You guessed it. Kathy went to school with her the next day, never to be seen again. That little doll was definitely a lavish gift from her loving heart.

Now our daughter is all grown up with four children of her own. Her younger daughter has a very tender heart for those less fortunate than herself. When the Samaritan's Purse Christmas Catalog arrives, she gets very excited. There are items that can be given with a cost as small as $7–$10 (as well as much more). The smaller items really light her fire. "I can do that, Mom! I can do that!"

Her family came to stay a few days with us to celebrate her Pawpaw's seventieth birthday. Knowing we were having a sizeable group of family members over, she asked if we could sell cookies to raise funds for Samaritan's Purse. Sure! So, she and I baked brownies and cookies, bagged them, and had them available for our guests to purchase at the birthday party. She was totally delighted at the prospects of raising funds. (Now, just *who* is going to turn down an adorable little girl with such a loving heart?)

Our nurses, schoolteachers, and builders dropped in dollar bills (and larger bills also) while complimenting her on her baked goods. At the end of the day, she had raised $73 for missions. She experienced absolute *Joy* (which is her middle name), as did the family. But best of all, somebody or somebodies somewhere got an unexpected hand up! Even small "alms" make a big difference. Selah!

In conclusion, no matter what we have or don't have, and no matter what we can do or cannot do, each of us can become a world-reaching woman. Even during a pandemic, secluded in our homes, we can give bit by bit consistently. Or we can give lavishly either locally or all around the world.

Equally as important as our giving is our prayer. We must ask the Lord to direct our gift to exactly the person who stands in need of that which we are impressed to give. As we listen to the promptings of the Holy Spirit and respond obediently, only heaven will reveal the impact of our "alms." How exciting to live in agreement with the God of the universe! Life doesn't get any better than this. Try it! World-reaching women are living a life of fulfillment.

Personal Response

- Assess your abilities.

  List three things that are easy and enjoyable for you to do. (The list is endless, but here are a few hints: baking, sewing, drawing, typing, painting, crafting, hosting, befriending, gift-giving, shopping for shut-ins, card sending, encouraging words by phone, text, etc.)

1. _____

2. _____

3. _____

Now list three activities that you cannot do well or that just outright annoy you. To avoid frustration, stay away from these.

1. _____

2. _____

3. _____

- Assess your availability.

  What are some ways you can use the above-mentioned abilities to help others?

1. _____

2. _____

3. _____

- Assess your possessions.

  What do you possess in an excessive amount? (Dishes, Christmas decorations, books, shoes, jewelry, furniture, clothes.)

  _____

  _____

  _____

  Check around to see who could benefit from your sharing these items you don't use.

  _____

  _____

  _____

- Assess your personal growth.

  Are there abilities you *wish* you could do better? How about taking a class to learn more? Maybe you could take it with someone else to build a friendship.

  Write your plan:

  _____

  _____

  _____

Prayer

Dear Father in heaven,

I come to You with a grateful heart. I am blessed beyond measure. Everything that I enjoy comes from Your gracious hand. I thank You for eyes to see the beauty of Your creation. I thank You for the privilege of living in a country where I have more than enough of everything I need. I thank You for my family and friends.

I thank You for the things that I can do. Show me how to serve You and love others with each ability. Help me not to get stymied by focusing on things I cannot do.

Today I come to You in surrender. I place myself, my abilities, and my inabilities at Your command. Open my eyes to those around me who need to be valued, loved, and encouraged. Value others through my care. Love others through my acts of kindness. Encourage others through my words.

I give You freedom to make me light in dark places and love in lonely places. Should You ask for a lavish gift, give me faith to trust Your leadership and to say "yes."

From this day forward, I ask You to so direct my life that it may be characterized by Your love, never greed or selfishness.

Thank You for hearing my prayer. Use me as You see fit. I love You, Lord Jesus.

Amen.

CHAPTER NINE

THE UNNAMED

Woman Caught in Adultery

But Jesus went to the Mount of Olives. Now early in the morning He came again into the temple, and the people came to Him; and He sat down and taught them. Then the scribes and Pharisees brought to Him a woman caught in adultery. And when they had set her in the midst, they said to Him, "Teacher, this woman was caught in adultery, in the very act. Now Moses, in the law, commanded us that such should be stoned. But what do You say?" This they said, testing Him, that they might have something of which to accuse Him. But Jesus stooped down and wrote on the ground with His finger, as though He did not hear. So when they continued asking Him, He raised Himself up and said to them, "He who is without sin among you, let him throw a stone at her first." And again He stooped down and wrote on the ground. Then those who heard it, being convicted by their conscience, went out one by one, beginning with the oldest even to the last. And Jesus was left alone, and the woman standing in the midst. When Jesus had raised Himself up and saw on one but the woman, He said to her, "Woman, where are those accusers of yours? Has no one condemned you?" She said, "No one, Lord." And Jesus said to her, "Neither do I condemn you; go and sin no more."

John 8:1–11

Drop the Stone

I was sure the wrong I had done
Was known by exactly *no one.*
But there were those I did not see
Looking with condemnation at me.
They came for me with evil intent, against my will,
Dragged into public view I went.
Now others knew the wrong I had done
As I appeared before God's Son.
He knew the payment for my wrong,
But with compassion said, "Drop the stone."
My accusers left the scene one by one,
Convicted by the wrong *they* had done.
Jesus stood before me with forgiveness and care
But warned me not to go back *there.*
Oh, my love for Him does abound
As I praise Him for writing that day on the ground.

Caught in the Act of Adultery

Author's Note: I considered ignoring this passage for obvious reasons. Yet, after discussing my ideas for this book with a good friend and writer, I was encouraged to include this chapter. Since I was taught early in life to heed trusted advice, I decided to include this difficult scenario. Then one morning, quite unexpectedly, I woke up with my mind flooded with ideas about this passage. While the thoughts and emotions of this woman are not recorded, we can "put ourselves in her shoes" and imagine what her frightful day was like based on what we are told in the Scriptures and what we know about others who made similar life choices.

Her Story

We are told nothing about this unnamed woman with the exception of her wrongdoing. She was caught committing adultery. We can only imagine circumstances that would lead to such a discovery and accusation. Where were she and her partner found? Had she been coerced into this behavior? Was this a common occurrence? We don't know if she was involved in "the world's oldest profession" or if she was used once as a part of the Pharisee's attempt to discredit Jesus publicly. When we meet her in the Scripture, she is being humiliated. Whether she was caught involved in her usual "job" or trapped with evil intent by scheming men, her personage was being totally disregarded. She was being dragged against her will into the temple, the house of worship, with her accusers shouting forth her sin to everyone present. She must have been mortified and deathly afraid. What would the religious community think, say, or do? Would they recommend the death penalty by stoning? Was her life about to end? It was in this horrifying circumstance that she met Jesus. His response to her was not what she feared.

Digging Deeper

Jesus was teaching in the temple early in the morning. Perhaps He was in the courtyard since there was soil available to Him. As always, many people had come to hear Him with honorable intent: to learn and to worship. There were also scribes and Pharisees who showed up with quite different motivations. You may recall that these were the religious authorities of the day who were not impressed with Jesus' new teaching. They were sticklers for enforcement of the Jewish laws, all six-hundred-plus of them. Jesus was proposing concepts of grace, forgiveness, and turning the other cheek. These ideas ran contrary to the Jewish law that dictated punishment for every small infraction or failure. Disgruntled, the religious leaders dogged Jesus' every move. Throughout His entire earthly ministry, they confronted Him, refuting His teaching and challenging His actions. They never gave up being adversarial. On this day, they came to disrupt and cast dispersion on His teaching right in front of His followers. It was in this setting that several of them came dragging a woman they said they had *caught in the act of committing adultery*.

That statement, *caught in the act*, raises several questions in my mind. Since a person cannot commit adultery alone, where was the other person? Yes, where was the man involved? In what place was this couple engaged in sexual activity that provided access for onlookers? Normally, people who are "fooling around" seek privacy. And where were the Pharisees? What were they doing? Were they out looking for someone—anyone—who was involved in something—anything—they themselves would never admit doing?

Jesus had His plan for that day. He was doing what He always did: instructing and enlightening His followers when, quite unexpectedly, several men stormed in. They were dressed in garments typically worn by the Pharisees. They were dragging a frightened, bedraggled woman and demanding Jesus' attention. They threw the woman down before Him. They were probably shouting, calling attention to the woman and to themselves: "Look at this woman. She was committing adultery. We saw her. Her actions are sinful and punishable by death."

Rather than responding to these religious zealots with outrage, Jesus remained calm. He quietly leaned forward and wrote something on the ground with His finger. The zealots continued shouting at Him: "What do You say, rabbi? Should we stone her now as Moses commanded?"

Again, unruffled, Jesus stood to face them. He did not refute Moses' law, and neither did He agree that the woman should be stoned. Instead, He said, "He who is without sin among you, let him throw a stone at her first." Then He wrote on the ground again.

Whatever it was that Jesus wrote, certainly "cut to the chase." It immediately convicted the men "by their own consciences." Their own sins were brought to mind. They became aware that Jesus knew about *their* wrongdoings. They realized they were just as guilty as the woman they brought before Him. One by one, they left the scene.

The Bible does not record what Jesus wrote on the ground that day. Some speculate that it could have been the names of women these accusers had been involved with, or He possibly listed some of their other sinful deeds. Regardless, the accusers drifted away one by one, from the oldest to the youngest, until the woman was left alone with Jesus.

What a sigh of relief this must have brought to this unnamed woman! She was not going to die, at least not that day, and not at their hands. But with her accusers gone, she was left alone in her guilt and shame, trembling with fear, to face Jesus! *What will He say? What will He do? For what punishment will He call?*

Once again, Jesus' response was unexpected. His manner and words dissolved her fears. "Where are your accusers?" He asked. "Did any of them condemn you?" "No, Lord, not one," she answered. "Neither do I," He assured her.

Surely these words brought her immediate relief. No doubt, she was aware that her sexual misconduct was morally wrong and contrary to the law of Moses. She never expected to get caught but to remain unknown to all others, except for the man involved. (Let's not forget him.) How terrified she had to have been when the zealots dragged her into the public arena, broadcasting her sin. Surely fear and guilt gripped her soul. Yet Jesus showed forgiveness and love, not by excusing her wrongdoing, but by absolving her of shame and guilt and by giving her new direction. He extended mercy to her, encouraged her to go on her way, and cautioned her to follow Him with a warning to "go and sin no more."

Selah. She came there guilty and left forgiven. She came afraid and left comforted. She went on her way, praising Jesus for His mercy extended to her. Selah!

In stark contrast to Jesus' love and compassion for the woman, the Pharisees' purpose was to ensnare Jesus by His own words and actions and to prove Him a fraud. In their attempt to enforce their laws, they opposed Jesus' teaching continually. On this day, they were purposefully seeking to set a trap for Jesus. They figured if He told the crowd not to stone the woman, He would be dishonoring the laws of Moses. On the other hand, if He declared her guilty and approved her stoning, He would be violating His own teachings of mercy, love, and forgiveness. The trap was set. Either way, He was caught! Oh, but wait. Not so! He was able to avoid their snare by writing something—known only to her accusers—that convicted their conscience of *their own* wrongdoing.

Like the Pharisees, we tend to view our wrongdoings as *not so bad*, while those of others might be seen as totally evil. Proverbs 6:16–19 gives us a picture of God's view of wrongdoing. That passage states that there are six things that God hates, seven that are an abomination to Him.

1. A proud look.
2. A lying tongue.
3. Hands that shed innocent blood.
4. A heart that devises wicked plans.
5. Feet that are swift in running to evil.
6. A false witness who speaks lies.
7. One who sows discord among brethren.

This is strong language. It is clearly stated that God deplores these deeds. Apparently, lying is high on the list since it is mentioned twice. We offend God Himself when we stir up conflict between believers. God hates our gossiping mouth or arrogance as much as He hates evil scheming or attacking and/or killing another person. Selah. Whoa! Think that over! He is holy. All wrongdoing is an affront to Him. He doesn't look at evil on an ascending and descending scale as we tend to do; therefore, all these acts are equally offensive to Him.

Consider these scriptures. They speak to this issue very clearly. James 4:17 states, "Therefore, to him who knows to do good and does not do it, to him it is sin." First John 5:17 says, "All unrighteousness is sin." This leaves no doubt. *All* our disobedience and transgressions cause Him grief.

Like the Pharisees, we, too, can be aware of another person's sinful deeds and think, *Oh, no, I would never do that!* We might also pick up proverbial stones of accusation, judgment, or arrogance and cast them at someone. However, if we follow Jesus' example, we should respond calmly, with care and concern. In other words, we, too, must *drop the stone. Instead of being self-righteous, we pray. We love. We forgive. We stand beside. We encourage. We befriend.*

Someone reading these pages might be thinking, *I am guilty of sexual sin*—either previously or ongoing—*and I deserve its consequences. I am tormented by the memories. My guilt haunts me day after day. I cannot seem to forgive myself.*

The sin might be *adultery* (sexual involvement with a married person), *fornication* (sexual involvement with an unmarried person), *abortion* (killing the unborn), *homosexuality* (sexual involvement with a same-sex partner), *pornography* (poisoning one's eyes or mind with perversion), and more. None of these acts classify you as beyond help. The Bible clearly states:

"Therefore, if anyone is in Christ, he is a new creation; old things have passed away; behold, all things have become new" (2 Corinthians 5:17).

No matter what you have done or how many times you have done it, you can have a new start. You can become a completely new person when you accept Jesus as Lord and Savior.

In explaining this concept to children, I used to tell them that God changes you from the inside out. No, your eyes don't change color. Your nose doesn't change shape. You don't grow four inches taller. However, you change on the inside. You have a new relationship with God. You think differently.

By reading the Bible, you have a new view of God and His ways. What you like changes, and what you dislike changes. So does what you love and what you hate. You develop a loving attitude toward other people. God is your Father. You have a new family of believers. These benefits and so many more are available to you. Call out to Jesus. He will not turn you away.

John 6:37 states, "All that the Father gives Me will come to Me, and the one who comes to Me I will by no means cast out."

Come to Him today. Pour your heart out to Him. Tell Him what you have done and how you feel about it. Ask for His forgiveness. He will give you a new beginning and a changed life. His arms are outstretched to *you*. When He stretched out His arms and died on the cross, He yelled, "It is finished!" That meant the debt for *all sin* was *paid in full* so that we do not have to pay the penalty for our own sins. He wants to be your compassionate, loving Savior, your guide, and your friend from now and throughout all eternity.

Just pray, "Lord Jesus, if this is true, prove it to me. I want forgiveness and a new beginning. I want a clean slate. You are my only hope. I have tried to change and failed. I need You. Forgive me. Save me. I want You to be my Lord. I want to obey You."

If you prayed this sincerely from your heart, remember this date. This is the day you became a member of God's forever family. Give Him praise! Tell a believer about your decision. Find a church that teaches God's Word. Read the Bible, especially the Gospels. Learn Jesus' ways and follow His example.

I have one final "furry little rabbit" to chase: As previously mentioned, we tend to rate wrongdoing on a scale. Some we classify as totally evil while others we consider not as bad, the ones that give us a struggle, we may give free pass and not consider them as harshly as we do the infractions of others. Yet, according to the contents of Proverbs 6 that we just discussed, all transgressions are motivated by evil intent and are offensive to God Himself. With that in mind, I find the term "hate crime" to be quite a misnomer. To me, *all* crimes are hate crimes. Have you ever known anyone to break down a door to violate another person's privacy motivated by kindness? Have you ever seen a house, business, or car defaced by graffiti and/or foul language motivated by goodwill? Do people rob others of valuable goods motivated by a sense of benevolence? What about acts of battery, stabbing, or slaying? Are these deeds motivated by compassion? Certainly *not*! It is when greed, malice, jealousy, and hatred are allowed to build up in the heart that a person has the impetus to carry out lawless and cruel deeds. So, how can this be corrected?

With a heart transplant! No, not a physical removal of the vital organ that pumps blood throughout the human body. It is the removal of the heart (the core of our being) naturally filled with selfishness, greed, malice, and hate that changes both attitude and actions. As the power of our triune God is allowed to implant a new heart, one filled with kindness, compassion, benevolence, and respect that desires will be changed from hatred to love. Yes, a heart transplant! That is the cure for hate crime, *all* crime!

Now, let's give consideration to the characters involved in this story and how their actions can be used to impact our lives.

The Unnamed Woman

She is forever known as "the woman caught in adultery." What a label! At least her name was not attached to that reputation. She paid a heavy price: caught and humiliated. Thankfully, she met Jesus and experienced His compassion and mercy. Assuredly, her life was never the same. No matter what road we travel, Jesus is always there to forgive and restore. He accepts and forgives all who come to Him, no matter the past. Selah!

No matter what road we travel, Jesus is always there to forgive and restore.

The Accusers

These men came with predisposed opinions about Jesus and the woman. Yet, they appeared totally unconcerned about the wrongdoing of the man also involved in adultery. Even after witnessing the power and compassion of Jesus, there is no indication the hearts of these men were softened. So, what do we take away? When we encounter people with an unchangeable mindset, we should be kind to them as Jesus was. Once we realize those people have no intention of changing, we should withdraw from the encounter. Continue to pray for the person. Give the Holy Spirit time to soften their heart and will. Then continue to reach out to others who will listen. Perhaps the resistant person will be approachable at another time.

Jesus

Jesus remained calm and unshaken despite the mob's interruptions and accusations. He had an agenda for that day, but He was not so tied to His plans that He could not see the plight of one unnamed woman. He adjusted His plans for her sake and changed her life. What an example He set for us. As we study His ways recorded in the Gospels, we see His footprints left for us to walk in and follow.

Personal Response

Are you more likely to be
☐ condemning or ☐ forgiving?

Do you face unexpected occurrences in life with
☐ anger or ☐ calmness?

Are you ☐ comfortable or ☐ uncomfortable dealing
with the wrongdoings of others?

Prayer

Dear Lord Jesus,

Thank You for giving me Your example of handling interruptions. Certainly, I need to grow in Your likeness by showing kindness, patience, and forgiveness. Help me never to show forth harshness or arrogance to those in need. I need Your calm demeanor. I need Your love. I need Your Holy Spirit to control my words and actions as I attempt to show Your ways to others. Forgive me for my failures of the past. Guide me day by day to be sensitive to those around me who need Your care. I love You and desire to follow in Your footsteps. Amen.

Afterword

A brief anecdote involving my grandmother.

As I reflected on Jesus' demeanor in this story, I remembered my grandmother, Mama Pittard. She was always calm and Christlike. She never shouted and never raised her voice in anger. I remember one summer day when my cousins and I were visiting her home. Mama Pittard was sitting by a window inside the house, sewing, pedaling away at her old Singer sewing machine. We, grandchildren, were entertaining ourselves by chasing each other around the inside of her house. It was constructed with a core in the middle that really did lend itself to being a racetrack.

After we ran several laps around the homemade track, Mama Pittard calmly declared, "If you children run through here one more time, I'm gonna get ya." Of course, we paid absolutely no attention to the warning and ran another lap. The next time we got to the room where she was sewing, she was standing there waiting for us. She stopped our little train by catching the first one in line, giving a small *pop* on the backside, then proceeded to do the same for each of us. We were shocked enough by the harmless *whack* to curtail our train and go on to another playful activity.

This was so typical of my grandmother. She was very calm. My mother (her daughter) said she could not remember her mother ever raising her voice for any reason. Selah! My children can't say that about me. How about yours? If Mama Pittard made a statement, she meant it. If she made a rule, she enforced it calmly.

Perhaps her example can give us hope in growing in Christlikeness as we react to life's continual unforeseen interruptions. It's a goal to strive to attain, but I doubt I will ever rise to her level.

CONCLUSION

There is no denying that there are women who have become high achievers. They have gained great accomplishments, and their names are known worldwide. However, they are relatively few compared to the millions who are only known by those in a small sphere of influence; yet, are faithful wives, mothers, employees, and more. Lives are lived doing the ordinary, the routine, the unnoticed.

Mortar Matters was written for those women known by relatively few: those who tirelessly give of themselves to care for, provide for, and nourish others. While this lifestyle has its own rewards, it can become discouraging; so much so that one may feel invisible. Family, friends, and coworkers mean no harm as they expect the fulfillment of these roles without their expression of honor. However, we know that *all* people need to feel valued. In relating these stories of unnamed women, Jesus conveyed the value He placed on those unknown by the masses.

In a variety of ways, He demonstrated His love for the individual others ignored. He crossed ethnic and cultural barriers to be there for *one*. He planned His day to be there for *one*. He gave time and effort to get to that *one*. He met the *one* at their time of deepest need. He assigned a term of endearment to *one*. He met the need of *one*. He showed compassion to *one*. He touched, healed, and even resurrected *one*. Most definitely, He showed us *one* matters and that expressions of care to *one* can be the unseen *mortar that matters* to turn one's life around.

Does mortar really matter?

Never have I seen anyone admire a house or any other man-made edifice and exclaim, "What a terrific job that mortar is doing!" Yet, mortar is the exact substance that holds the building together. There, unnoticed yet sturdy and dependable, the mortar prevents the wall or building from collapsing. Yes! *Mortar Matters*!

Several years ago, my brother-in-law had a rather expensive house built. The exterior had columns and accent walls of the trendy "stacked stone" look. *Mortar Matters* was already germinating in my mind, so I examined the "stacked stones" as best I could. While they appeared "stacked," deep inside, there was mortar holding them in place. That unseen, unheralded substance was performing its task. As I contemplated this idea, a parallel came to mind: unseen, unheralded deeds also matter. I recalled deeds that have impacted my life over a wide span of years.

Mrs. Gregory was the first Sunday School teacher I can remember. She was quiet by nature. She loved the Lord and teaching from the Bible (way back when flannel board figures were used). She was faithful and well prepared. The day I will never forget is the day we girls were invited to her home. She had goodies for us. To the best of my memory, we girls were allowed to get our hands into cookie dough. Among other things, we played in her backyard. Before we left her home, she allowed us to keep an apron she had made for each of us. I have kept mine over the years. The fond memories of that day still bring delight! Yes! *Mortar Matters!*

At our first pastorate in Fort Pierce, Florida, there was a most gifted yet unpretentious lady named Mrs. Colby. Her nickname was "Billie." She affectionately called me "Miss January," and I affectionately called her "Miss Silly Billie." She was more gifted and godlier than I ever thought about being. She was also quite an artist. I would go to her with ideas for bulletin boards, seasonal decorations, or art for themed banquets or lady's events. She would come up with fantastic art that would make the ideas vivid in our minds. It was this talented lady who wrote me a note I'll never forget! In a card thanking me for something, she said, "If I were young again, I'd want to grow up to be like you. You do everything so well!" Whoa! That was off the charts! I grew up in an era when doing your best was expected and not necessarily verbally or monetarily rewarded. Doing right brought its own reward and satisfaction! You'd better believe this was a note to be cherished for life! It was the beginning of an "encouragement file" I still have. When life gets tough, I can go there to remember there have been times I blessed someone and "got it right." The file has grown to two and still brings a lift whenever I need it. Remember, it all began with a single, heart-felt expression of appreciation that has encouraged me for over forty years! Does *Mortar Matter*? Oh, I'd say so!

It was early February of 2011 when my ninety-one-year-old mother fell and was taken to the local hospital. It was determined that the fall resulted from heart failure. She was losing ground rapidly. Due to protocol, hospital officials decided she should be moved to the closest hospice facility. By that time, she was fragile and extremely weak. I thought the idea of moving her was outright crude and heartless. Rules are rules! So, they transported her by ambulance. Charlene, my sister, and I rode together to the hospice facility. Immediately upon our arrival (while Mother was being settled into bed there), hospice personnel reached out to us with *extreme* love and compassion. One thing they asked us was, "Would you like some cake?" I would have dismissed the idea, but my sister said, "That sounds good." Boy, am I glad she did! Momentarily, we were served some of the most delicious and moist chocolate sheet cake ever! Absolutely divine! That cake treated our bodies and diverted our minds from the sorrow we were facing. I have no idea who made that cake. I can imagine someone poking their head into a Sunday School class, saying, "It is our week to bake cakes for the local hospice. Who will volunteer? Okay, Grace, Margaret, and Linda, have your cakes here by 9 a.m. Tuesday morning, and I'll take them over. Now, do remember to pray for those who will be ministered to through this outreach."

I believe I will meet that unnamed, unknown lady who "did what she could" as she treated our taste buds to unforgettable chocolate cake while our spirits were grieving. That was part of her storing up treasures in heaven. She may never speak in public or have her name in lights, but "what she could" truly ministered to two heartbroken daughters that day. Yes, *Mortar Matters*!

Another question was asked of us that day: "Do you want the service of our chaplain?" Both our husbands were on their way. Charlene's husband is a strong Christian who has taught Bible classes for years. My Jerry, minister for "forever," was called and was en route. Once again, sis responded and said, "We'll take what you have." I don't remember the name of the precious lady who came in, met us, and hugged us warmly. Then she sat by Mom, singing "How Great Thou Art" as we finished our cake. By the way, that was one of my mother's very favorite songs! What a God moment!

Mother left us and took her flight to her eternal home within one hour of arriving at the hospice. Our hearts were broken. Mrs. Chaplain was there to comfort, to hug, and to allow us to spill tears and drip noses all over her clothes. I apologized profusely to her, but she assured me that was why she was there. She was being who she was, doing what she could do. Surely, I will never forget her kindness.

Does *Mortar Matter*? Oh, yes! These deeds mentioned are known by very few individuals, yet they brought immense comfort to two aching hearts. I believe these are "cups of water" that will not lose their reward. Jesus said if we make small gestures in His name, He sees! He keeps the records! He will reward! (Matthew 10:42)

So, you may ask, "How can I be the *mortar that matters* in the life of another. Let's consider five ways we could make that happen.

1. **Be Yourself**

   Take a candid look in the mirror. Who are you? What words would describe you? (Creative, sensitive, boring, musical, organized, crafty, outgoing, energetic, a leader, a follower, verbal, quiet, studious, listener, nurturing.) What makes you laugh or cry? What motivates you? Who are your heroes? What abilities do you have? Be honest. (Draw, write, play an instrument, bake, garden, host, befriend, work hard, computer savvy, photography, and more.)

2. **Embrace Yourself**

   After you have looked at who you are and what you can do, embrace it. Give thanks to God for all that He has included in "who you are." God made you exactly the way He wanted you to be, and He is very capable of using you with what He has given you. No more and no less.

3. **Surrender Yourself**

   Acknowledge any natural abilities and strong interests you have been made aware of. Consciously commit them to be used by the Holy Spirit of God to bless others. Even if they seem minimal to you, surrendered, they can be used, anointed, and multiplied for His glory!

4. Fill Yourself

As you stay in the Word, it will give you examples and ideas of how "this Christianity thing works." As you become more and more like Jesus, your desire to serve will grow. You will become sensitive to the needs around you. As you pray, the Lord will enhance your creativity, guide you to those in need, give you new ideas, and fill you with His love. As was mentioned earlier, "When you are filled, you spill."

5. Empty Yourself

When you are full, you flow! So, fill up with more and more knowledge about your interests and abilities. Become full, and don't be shy to flow. It may seem slow and small at first, but be assured your flow will grow. The Word promises that when we give, we will receive (Luke 6:38). God's supply of everything never runs out. We are promised that when we give, the "stock" will be replenished so that we give again! How exciting!

As I have mentioned previously, we have no way of knowing how meaningful a deed of kindness will be to another individual. When I worked in public school, several of us formed a prayer group. Some years we had a sizable group, ten, fourteen, or more. Schedules changed, assignments changed so much so that one year, for most of our before-school prayer meetings, it was only my friend,

Ester, and me. We had a loving, caring, worshipful time together.

In previous years, just before Christmas break, we would plan to come in earlier than usual, bring food, and share in a little Christmas celebration. The year that it was just Ester and me, I figured there would be no celebration. Much to my surprise, when I arrived and opened the door to our meeting room, there was a beautiful table with food, decorations, lights, and all things festive. Ester, who loves fancy and is a gifted decorator, had come in to set all this up *for me*! Whoa! I am still excited to recall that. She was being herself, doing what she could do, and I am still blessed just to remember that morning. Oh yes! *Mortar Matters!*

Here's one more story. Same school, just another time. A young man came in as a substitute teacher. I saw unusual ability and potential in him. I encouraged him verbally. When he was leaving that assignment, I wrote him a note and then completely forgot about it. Several years later, I met up with a lady who had run into him at her church. He was in town to visit. He asked her if I was still around. He wanted me to know that he still had the note. Also, he was completing his studies to become a classroom teacher. Wow! I had *no idea* what that tiny note of encouragement would mean to that young man. Surely, *Mortar Matters!*

Mortar: the unnoticed, often unseen material that bonds one substance to another. (My personal definition.) Isn't that the mental imagery of why we are left here on Earth? As growing and learning children of God, we hold to His truth with one hand while extending the other hand to others, those in need of Him. In effect, we become the *mortar* or the substance to connect people below to God above. My grandmother used to sing, "Hold to God's unchanging hand. *Build your life on things eternal.* Hold to God's unchanging hand." That's it! We *are* here to grow in His likeness and to pass His truth on to others. We, ordinary individuals, walk through our everyday life, stretching one hand *up* and one hand *out*. As we use our days to influence others to accept Jesus and His way, our lives are built on *things eternal*. We are literally helping to populate heaven. Nothing is more important. Our outreach, though known by few, will matter for all eternity. Oh, yes! Truly, *Mortar Matters*!

ENDORSEMENTS

God placed Jan Brown (AKA Mama Jan) in my life at a time when I needed a mentor, mother figure, and a friend. I was a young educator in Georgia, and she worked alongside me as an experienced paraprofessional. We clicked easily; we shared a common love for the Lord, a deep faith, and a desire to help and serve others. Together we started a Bible study/prayer time with the staff where we taught. We worked hard to reach our students where they were and had high expectations for what they could achieve. I am so proud of Jan and excited to read this book. She has been such an inspiration in my life. I am sure she will be the same for you, her reader, as well.

—Kelly Janes

I was in the first grade with Jan Brown, then separated only to reunite in high school. It was during those high school years that a dear friendship developed and has become more precious over many years. I feel God has gifted Jan with writing ability, and I am excited for it to reach book form. I am praying that God will continue to use her and this book to help change countless lives for His glory.

—Connie Peppers

Jan Brown will be the first to say her most important role in life has been that of a God-fearing child of God. Her other roles include wife, mother, grandmother, Bible teacher, women's ministry leader, hostess, and children's ministry leader. She has also taught preschool, kindergarten, and first grade. The daughter of a devout Christian family, Jan made her profession of faith as a young child and has followed Jesus throughout her life. After meeting her husband in college, she has supported him in ministry in six churches in Florida and Georgia. Jan and her husband, Jerry, are parents of two adult children who have together blessed them with seven grandchildren.

—Maxine Thomas

Jan Brown and my late wife, Carol, met as college freshmen. Jan married Jerry Brown (same last name) and exchanged visits, calls, and letters with us through the years as they served as pastor and pastor's wife and raised a son and a daughter. A year before Carol died, the Browns helped us move. They also were with me when Carol passed. Jan is a good writer and has poured many of her life experiences into this book. I enjoyed its content. She is good at exhorting folk to follow Jesus. I believe this book will help many because Jan has offered "her broken bottle of precious ointment" as a gift to the Lord.

—Steve Crain

It is no surprise that Jan would write about unnamed women in the Bible. As a pastor's wife, she had years of teaching and listening to others. Jan and Jerry have faithfully served in churches in Georgia and Florida. There, Jan has loved and encouraged other women. "Mortar Matters" beautifully reminds us all that Jesus sees the everyday, ordinary women, the unnamed women, and cares about the struggles of our lives. It is my prayer that many women will read Jan's words and be drawn to a strong walk with the Jesus she loves.

—Carol Plumlee

For response and comments
to the author, you can email her at
mortarmatters@gmail.com